ADVANCE PRAISE

"Brooke Brittain reminds us that the strongest leaders are the ones who keep their hearts open. *Between Grief and Grit* shows what optimism and toughness really looks like—it's courage in motion."
—JON GORDON,
18x best-selling author of *The Energy Bus* and *The Carpenter*

———

"Brooke Brittain doesn't just write about grit—she embodies it. *Between Grief and Grit* is a profile in courage and a beacon for anyone who's ever led through the storm instead of waiting for it to pass."
—DAMON WEST,
best-selling author of *The Coffee Bean*

———

"Brooke Brittain has artfully mapped the landscape between grief and grit, showing us that during times of trauma, leaders need not choose between self-care and caring for others. Learning to do both together can take us beyond mere resilience to new growth, greater strength, and deeper understanding."
—DR. JIM BRENNAN, PHD,
human performance specialist and expert in emotional intelligence; author of *The Art of Becoming Oneself*

———

"Brooke Brittain tells the truth many leaders live but rarely say—sometimes you have to lead while you're hurting. *Between Grief and Grit* is raw, real, and full of heart. Brooke doesn't just write about strength; she offers hard-won wisdom that helps leaders keep leading with love and courage, even in the dark."

—ANDY REID,
Super Bowl-winning head coach, Kansas City Chiefs

———

"Brooke Brittain is the embodiment of a citizen-soldier. When she was needed, she was there—leading with conviction, following fearlessly, and executing every mission with a standard of excellence. She carried that same blueprint into coaching and teaching, using it to build winning teams. When faced with adversity, her true character was revealed: champion. In *Between Grief and Grit,* Brooke shares that journey with authenticity and offers the practical tools she has relied on in every arena she has served."

—BRIGADIER GENERAL (RET.) JOHN HAFLEY,
US Army

BETWEEN GRIEF AND GRIT

BETWEEN GRIEF AND GRIT

A Flashlight for Leaders Navigating the Dark

Brooke Brittain

BETWEEN GRIEF AND GRIT
A Flashlight for Leaders Navigating the Dark

Cover Design by Abigael Elliott
Interior Layout and Design by Brittany Becker
Editorial Team: Karen Rowe, Anna Bolch, Ginny Glass, Kiska Carr

ISBNs:
Ebook: 979-8-89165-415-0
Paperback: 979-8-89165-416-7
Hardcover: 979-8-89165-417-4

Published by:
Streamline
Kansas City, MO

*For the ones who lead in the dark: the soldiers, the coaches,
the teachers, the first responders, the "sheepdogs,"
the community leaders, caretakers, and commanders
who hold everyone else together
while quietly trying not to fall apart.*

*For the ones who keep showing up when it hurts,
who steady their teams when their own hands are shaking,
who carry grief in one hand and grit in the other,
and keep leading, even when they're bleeding.*

*This light is for you.
And for me.
The book I once needed
has become my gift of grief.*

CONTENTS

PART 1: THE DARK

PART 2: THE LIGHT

PART 3: THE FIGHT

FOREWORD

By Monte "Sarge" Mills
For Brooke. My hero.

OPERATION IRAQI FREEDOM, *2003*
There are people the war sends into your life, and there are people the war sends into your soul. For me, Private Brooke Brittain was both. Operation Iraqi Freedom 2003, the first push of the war. I was her team leader. She was my driver. And together we rolled into the dark with nothing but a paper map, a worn-out Humvee, and a whole lot of prayer disguised as confidence.

People talk a lot about leadership these days. They write books, host podcasts, give TED Talks about it. But real leadership, the kind you don't volunteer for, is what shows up when the lights go out and you've got somebody else's life in your hands. And out there in that desert, where the horizon burned green under night vision and the world rumbled like God dragging furniture across the sky, I learned this truth: Leaders aren't defined by rank. They're defined by who they become in the dark.

Brooke was steady in the kind of darkness that makes grown men tremble. She was young, sure, too young for the things we saw, but she carried a quiet grit and a soul-deep courage I recognized long before she did. Her hands never shook on the wheel. Her eyes stayed sharp. And when fear crawled up the back of your neck, she didn't panic. She leaned in.

She didn't know it then, but she was already becoming the kind of leader this book is written for. We didn't know what Shock and Awe would feel like until we lived it. We didn't know how loud silence could be. And we sure as hell didn't know how much one night can change a life.

I used to load up my M203 with flares when that darkness felt like it was closing in to send a streak of light into the sky just so I could see what we were about to face. Sometimes it revealed threats. Sometimes it revealed nothing. But it, the light, always revealed the truth. And that's exactly what this book does.

Between Grief and Grit is Brooke's flare into the night sky. A sudden wash of light. A moment of truth in the places most leaders avoid. A flashlight for the battles that don't make headlines but make or break the human spirit.

Most people never stand in a combat zone. Most leaders never carry a rifle. But every leader knows what it feels like to have people counting on them when they're running on fumes. That's what makes Brooke's story sacred.

She's walked through warzones, locker rooms, hospital hallways, funerals, and the quiet moments where your own breath betrays you, and she came back with something to share. Not theory. Not jargon. But wisdom carved out of the real fight: how to keep leading when you're bleeding. How to carry others when your own hands are shaking. How to find light when all you can see is the next inch in front of you.

When she told me she was writing this book, I wasn't surprised. This wasn't a project; it was a calling. For years, she had been carrying pieces of this inside her: the moral injuries, the scars, the guilt that tries to rewrite truth, and the flickers of hope that refuse to die.

And she packaged it all with courage and vulnerability in a way only a soldier-turned-coach-turned-warrior-of-the-human-heart can.

What you'll read here is not comfortable. It's not polished. It's real. It's the kind of real that saves people.

I've watched soldiers stand in the dark and whisper they're fine when their eyes say otherwise. I've watched coaches try to hold whole locker rooms together while their own hearts are breaking. I've watched leaders in every sector fight quiet battles no one else can see. And what Brooke gives you in these pages is a light bright enough, and honest enough, to guide them through.

If you're reading this, you probably lead someone. If you're breathing, you've probably been broken somewhere along the way. And if you're brave enough to keep going, to keep serving, to keep showing up, this book is for you.

Brooke, I couldn't be prouder of the soldier you were, the leader you've become, and the warrior you're still choosing to be, not because life was kind but because you refused to quit. You've taken the darkest parts of your story and turned them into a light that others can follow.

You were my driver once. Now you're driving a generation of leaders out of the darkness. So, to the reader, tighten your grip. Take a breath. Turn the flashlight on.

Forward, always.

MONTE "SARGE" MILLS
US Army Military Police Corps
Operation Iraqi Freedom 2003

A NOTE TO THE READER

I F YOU'RE HOLDING this book, chances are you've had to lead when things didn't go as planned. You've stood in rooms where something had broken and people were looking to you to steady the ground. You learned how to keep moving, how to show up, how to carry responsibility even when you weren't sure how to carry yourself.

This book comes from those places. These stories were written in the gap between what leaders are expected to do and what it actually feels like to do it. They aren't meant to impress or instruct. They're meant to tell the truth.

Some of what's here may resonate. Some ideas you may resist. Some chapters may never connect. Other concepts will.

You won't find answers to everything in these pages. I didn't. What I found instead were moments of clarity—small lights that helped me take the next step when I couldn't see very far ahead.

If this book offers anything, I hope it offers a reminder that you're not alone and the space to consider what helps you stay grounded in the work you've been called to do.

Chapter 1

THE WARRIOR'S TRIANGLE

HAVE YOU EVER noticed how quickly people think they know the answer to your problems when life gets hard? Some tell you to dig deeper and be stronger. Some tell you to lean harder on the people around you. Some tell you to trust God and wait.

Each of these holds real power. But when any one of them is treated as the only answer, something essential gets lost. I've learned that in places where getting it wrong had consequences: war zones, locker rooms, hospital rooms, and leadership roles where people were depending on me to stand when things were breaking.

Strength was never meant to come from one place. Separate them, and you weaken the structure. Hold all three, and you can stand firm. When pressure hits from every direction, a one-way approach won't carry you through real storms. Relying on a single source of strength is often how leaders collapse.

What holds is balance, which really comes from sharing the weight rather than carrying it alone. To stand when the storm hits, you need three things working together for real strength: the grit to fight, the people to hold the line beside you, and the faith to believe you're not fighting alone.

That balance—the power of self, squad, and spirit—is what keeps you strong. It's what I call *the Warrior's Triangle.* It's how I make sense of leadership under pressure: maximizing the power that each of them brings through supporting each other in their own way.

The triangle is more than just a metaphor; it's a functional structure that handles weight.

Engineers will tell you it's the strongest shape there is because it resists collapse under pressure. Each side distributes the weight. And that's exactly why leaders need it. Because when one side starts to weaken—when your sense of self cracks, your squad fractures, or your spirit struggles—the other sides can steady the load until you find your footing again.

Together, they make the whole strong. Together, they make you resistant to pressure. While each side is important, the real strength comes when they work together to handle the pressure.

SELF

When I was a young soldier, I attended my first noncommissioned officer academy—the Warrior Leadership Course. In the military, passing these academies isn't optional; they're the gates to your next rank. Failure of a test sends you home, and your career progression is done.

In Warrior Leadership Course, of all the tasks—leadership drills, written tests, field exercises—the one everyone whispered about was *land navigation.* Unlike the basics in boot camp, this was a little more advanced: plotting grid coordinates, using nothing but a map, a compass, and a protractor, then disappearing into the woods *alone.* Four points to find: find two and you fail, three to pass, four required to aim for excellence with the label exceeds standard.

Before we went out, the cadre gave us a safety briefing I'd never heard before: "It's been raining. The marshlands out here act like quicksand,

and they are dangerous right now. Stay out. If you hit soft soil and start to sink, stop. Back out the way you came. Don't test it."

I'd fought in deserts. I'd seen combat. But a swampy quicksand? That was new.

The test day was hot and steamy, with periodic rain coming down in sheets. I was off to a good start as I nailed my first two points with ease. I was feeling really good as I spotted my third coordinate post in the distance and hustled toward it—until my foot sank. Then my leg. Knee-deep in sucking mud, I grabbed a tree branch for balance and to slow the struggle that only seemed to make me sink deeper. Holding the flimsy tree branch, I froze as fear crept in. I wasn't sure whether my fear came from the risk of failure or bodily harm first, but as I held on to the branch, another fear crept in—the fear that I didn't know how to get out of this. I began to feel helpless.

And then I thought, *I want my mom.*

Not *I need to get out of this.*

Not *What's my escape plan?* Just *Mom.*

The irony? My mom's a wonderful, faith-filled woman, but she's not exactly the type to grab a rucksack and bail me out of this.

I caught myself being weak and mocked myself. *Mom's not here—what on earth is she going to do, Brooke? She's not coming. No one is. You're it.*

That was the pivot, the moment I stopped wishing for rescue and started moving. I freed my legs, backtracked to stable ground, got creative to find a new path, and found all four points. *Exceeds Standard.*

That lesson hit best because it was simple: When you're stuck and scared, your first instinct is to wish you weren't there and wait for rescue. But the moment you realize no one's coming, you move. You move because you *have* to.

Helplessness takes over when we forget our own strength. But when we turn inward first, we usually find we're already equipped for what's in front of us—more capable, more skilled, and more prepared than we believe. My win that day wasn't just finishing—it was realizing I was strong enough to get myself out of the mess I was in.

That's an important key to how we survive, and it's from there that we begin to thrive.

This theme runs deep in stories of leadership and resilience: No one is coming to save you. Not your mom, your boss, or your best friend. And, if they do, you'll never master the next level. And if you're always waiting for help, you'll never know what you're capable of until you're knee-deep in the mud with no one left to call but yourself.

SQUAD: THE FOXHOLE FEW

Some people call them confidants. I call them *foxhole friends.*

They are the people who can handle seeing you at your worst but still believe in you at your best. They'll sit beside you in your mess without judgment, but they know who you really are, and they'll hold you accountable when you need it. They're the ones you trust to have your back in the fight, even though the hardest battles are yours alone to face. They are your battle buddies when you are at war.

I'm humbled by how many foxhole friends God has given me through-out different seasons. In my darkest moments, I've chosen to share glimpses of the fight with the trusted few who I needed until I was stronger.

In 2009, I didn't tell anyone when I put my Glock in my mouth, and I struggled alone. Years later, after the murder of a student athlete, losing close friends to cancer, and a period of poorly managing my combat-related post-traumatic stress disorder (PTSD), all amid deep disconnection, I found myself very dark again. What I hadn't done before, but finally did then, was something simple and different: I shared my struggle with a foxhole friend. I still remember sitting at a lunch table, offering her tiny pieces of my inner war as I told her I could barely find the strength to get off the couch or even make it to work.

She prayed with me, right there, for the thoughts I'd shared and the struggles I was facing. It wasn't a miracle cure, but I learned this:

bringing the hidden darkness into the light makes the dark lose its power. And sharing it with someone who loves you enough to sit in the foxhole, if only for a moment, keeps you from feeling alone. That moment didn't erase the work I still had to do, but it freed me from shackles I had struggled to break alone.

Life gives us the friends we need at the times we need them, and in return, I aim to be that kind of friend for others. I guard those stories, those sacred spaces, those foxholes. My best foxhole friend is my wife. She's a police officer who's seen some of the ugliest things in the world, from homicide cases to internet crimes against children and undercover work in human trafficking. She does not have to share my experiences to understand that some situations just need a supportive friend when the world gets heavy.

No one is coming to save you, but that doesn't mean you fight alone. When you face challenges, the people in your foxhole don't carry you; they cover you, steady you, and help you keep fighting.

SPIRIT: UNSEEN ORDERS

Self-reliance keeps you moving. The foxhole few keep you from breaking alone. But the third leg of this triangle, *spirit*, keeps you guided. This was the hardest side of the triangle for me to trust and the one that took the longest to understand.

By *spirit*, I mean faith in motion, the part of you that stays open and responsive to God even if he feels far away. It's not blind belief; it's active trust. It's the awareness that even in silence, he's at work, moving pieces you can't yet see. And it's the courage to follow when he whispers your next step.

Years ago, during a deployment, I sat on the banks of the Jordan River in the town of Little Bethany, where Christ was baptized, praying to feel something again. I was numb from grief, loss, and the weight of leading in dark places. I rolled up my pants, stepped into the water, and prayed with everything I had. Across the river in Israel, I watched others being baptized, and I recognized that this was an incredibly holy space where Jesus had *physically* been baptized by John the Baptist. I splashed water on my face and begged God to let me *feel* His presence, which felt so far away. Perhaps this is dramatic, but I longed for a movie-like revival of my soul, a flood of feelings like comfort, passion, life, hope, inspiration, tears. *Something.* But nothing came.

At one of the holiest places on earth, praying for numbness to end, only to walk away feeling nothing, was one of the loneliest moments of my life, made heavier by how desperately I needed to feel something. Surely *here*, I thought, he would let me feel something, some sign he was near. Instead, I left more hopeless than when I arrived.

A few days later, on a mission in Aqaba, Jordan, I was doing my morning workout alone in the Red Sea when, out of nowhere, a thought surfaced: *I'm going to write a book with Jon Gordon.*

It wasn't dramatic or loud—it was a whisper. The kind that doesn't shake the air but shifts something inside you. I wasn't a writer. I had no plan. But the thought of writing a book with my favorite author made my heart smile for the first time in months. To think that my words could help someone get through in the same way *The Energy Bus* had impacted me felt like a spark of purpose in the middle of a sea of numbness. I didn't realize then that the whisper wasn't actually about writing a book with Jon Gordon—it was about obedience. I needed to start the journey that would eventually become this book.

Following that whisper led me down an unexpected path. I started writing, first an article for *Texas Coach Magazine*. From that came an invitation to speak at the Texas High School Coaches Association's Leadership Summit. Preparing for my first major stage—standing before a room of leaders I deeply admired, I prayed over what to share, wanting to honor the stage God had placed me on. I asked, *What could I possibly offer them that would truly serve their hearts?* But I didn't want the answer I received.

The answer came quietly at first. Then insistently. *February 24.*

I would be speaking at the Leadership Summit on February 24, 2020. February 24, 2009, marked the loss of the first soldier we lost in combat—a date etched into my life. That realization punched me in the gut, and I fought God on what I kept feeling him calling me to discuss that day.

Our community had recently been through multiple episodes of gun violence, and I watched leaders I love face trauma on our doorstep. It was already fully on my heart, and now I was being asked to stand before these leaders and open that door, exposed and vulnerable, as if this journey was the only one God wanted me to bring to the stage.

I didn't want to follow the call. I literally yelled out loud in defiance: "I do *not* want to talk about this." I pleaded: *Let me talk about coaching. Training. Leadership. Anything but—this.*

You will encounter more of my journey with February 24, and the loss it carries, later in this book. But this moment is not about that story itself. It is about obedience and faith in motion. On February 24, 2020, I told parts of *this* story for the first time, sharing the loss of a soldier in combat, the weight of darkness and disconnection, and the need to support coaches through trauma. The heart of that talk eventually led me to pursue my doctorate.

Today, at the time of writing, I'm a year away from completing my doctorate at Creighton University. My dissertation, *Between Grief and Grit: A Phenomenological Study on High School Coaches Leading Through Violent Loss*, aims to support what I was called to start that day. This book is my chance to share my personal lessons learned before I study others and eventually use both personal experience and academic, research-backed avenues to serve leaders in dark times.

When you listen to the spirit and let it guide you, all sorts of things will surprise you. I have learned that *some whispers are more like shouts.* Guess who spoke right after me at the Texas High School Coaches Leadership Summit that day? Yes, my favorite author/speaker, Jon Gordon. He was the first major encourager of my story as I stepped off stage, and the time I had to soak up his mentorship after my speech that day impacted me deeply. I did not write a book with Jon Gordon. But he was literally the first person to light up with enthusiasm and tell me I did awesome the moment I walked off the most vulnerable stage of my life. That's the thing about the spirit—God is working to connect dots that you don't even know exist yet. He brings the right people and the right moments, in the right order.

When I began mapping out this book, I reached out to Kathryn Gordon, Jon's wife, who had just opened their publishing company. Those relationships helped me learn more and find the right path for this journey. I could not have crafted this story on my own if I tried. This was God's writing.

God's plan has been bigger than mine, and he was not finished with this part of the story. On February 24, a day that had held me captive for so long, he continued aligning relationships that would become lasting friendships, mentorships, and sources of inspiration. As I stepped off the stage, a man approached Jon and me and said he had deeply connected with parts of my story and wanted to meet me. His name was Damon West. I had no idea that he would become one of the most inspirational people I would ever encounter. I am still humbled and grateful to say that Damon was the very first person to endorse this book.

Damon West, me, and Jon Gordon at THSCA Leadership Summit

Some call it luck. Others, coincidence. But I find the absolute *awe* in it as I see it for what it is: the answer to my numb prayer, in the form of a whisper from the same God who parted the Red Sea, now coming full circle and carrying me, step-by-step, into the work I was meant to do. Turning the hard and heavy into something that helps someone else. That's what the Spirit does. He doesn't send the rescue team; he whispers the next step. And if you keep moving toward his voice, you'll see he's been guiding you the whole way.

BUILT TO HOLD

The Warrior's Triangle isn't a catchy framework; it's a battle-tested survival structure.

- *Self:* This starts with radical ownership. You have to realize no one is coming to save you and the mission belongs to you alone.
- *Squad:* The Foxhole Few. The people beside you who will sit with you in the dark but won't let you live there.
- *Spirit:* Unseen Orders. Follow the whispers of God's Spirit faithfully. Trust the Commander who sees the whole field.

WARRIOR'S TRIANGLE

These aren't competing philosophies; they're *force multipliers*. Drop one, and your foundation tilts. Hold all three, and you can stand in any fight. The road ahead is where *Between Grief and Grit* begins to take shape.

These stories are not polished speeches or easy lessons that are universal—they're the flashlight itself exploring the dark. Each comes from a season when my own light dimmed, when leadership collided with trauma, and I had to find the next step before I could see the path. Some moments happened in combat. Others in locker rooms, hospitals, or hallways filled with grief. But in each, the balance between self, squad, and spirit was tested and rebuilt.

My hope is that as you read, you'll find pieces of your own story here and, somewhere between the grief and the grit, you'll feel less alone. To do that, we have to step into the dark.

PART 1

THE DARK

You can't fix what you can't see.
This is where the light first flickers—
when fear, guilt, and grief blur
the edges of who we are.
Before healing comes honesty;
before strength, sight.

Chapter 2

FEAR IN THE DARK

SHOCK AND AWE—the name given to the first wave of war in Iraq in March 2003, meant to crush the enemy in one overwhelming strike. One choice was given to Saddam Hussein's Iraqi Army: Surrender or die.

Most people watched it at home from their living rooms. I watched it in person—twenty years old, boots in the sand at the border of Iraq and Kuwait. I was just a private and a member of a small team, but in the eerie darkness of this night, I learned a powerful lesson on operating in darkness that would become clear to me years later as a leader in crisis.

Here's how it played out: Our Humvee sat in a 360-degree security perimeter, guarding against threats we couldn't see. We rotated in shifts: one soldier in the gunner's turret, one on the radio, one trying to rest, but the rest never came.

As I lay on the cot in front of our Humvee, I slept with my boots still on and my rifle tucked against my chest like a security blanket. Every crackle of the radio made my body tense. Somewhere beyond the berm, friends of mine were hunkered down, hoping to make it through the night without a firefight.

There's a photo from that night, taken through night vision goggles. It still feels unreal. The hazy green and gray from the night vision goggles changed shapes as bombs rumbled. The sky flickered in sync with the chaos, then went calm again. And all night, oil pipelines glowed in the distance as they burned.

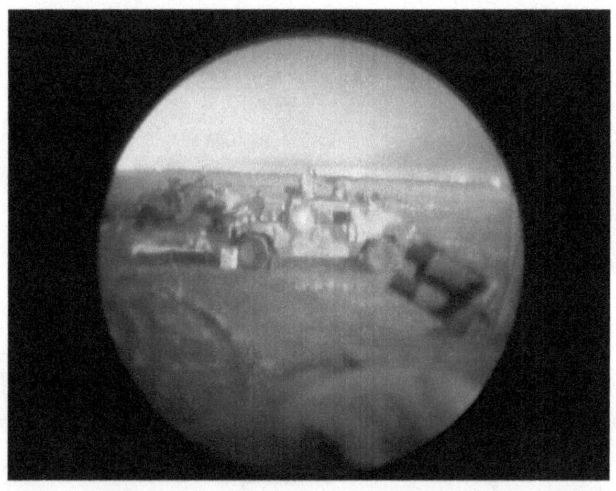

Shock and Awe. Kuwait/Iraq Border 2003. 302nd MP Company, First Platoon. (My Humvee is center.)

What that photo doesn't capture are the sounds. Gunfire echoing in short bursts. The crackle of radio traffic. Explosions that were too far off to be threatening, but the eerie rumbling gave no doubt about the massive destruction taking place across the land.

We maintained strict noise-and-light discipline to avoid being targeted—sitting in pure darkness, barely speaking among ourselves. The far-off rumbles were met with strange periods of silence and a tension that I can still feel every time I think of that night. You could taste adrenaline and know there was great danger in the distance yet find a strange peace because it was just beyond your reach—for the time being.

As a twenty-year-old kid from the suburbs, witnessing Shock and Awe in real life, I was scared that first night of the war—but not for the reasons you'd think. All night long, amid the bombs and gunfire, wild dogs yowled as they hit our C-wire perimeter, which was a barbed wire meant to slow or deter anyone approaching. I never saw the dogs that night. I only heard them: running, growling, hitting the wire, then scurrying back into the dark.

This is not a heroic war story. Private Brittain was *terrified* of the dogs.

Not the war. Not the enemy. Not the threat. Not the bombs or the gunfire. I was afraid of *the wild dogs.* I would lie on my cot, hugging my rifle, eyes wide open, staring into the dark while hoping the dogs wouldn't get through the wire and reach me before I could see them and fight back.

When the sun rose the next morning, I had my own secret mission in addition to fighting Saddam's army—to find the monstrous dogs that had terrorized me all night. I needed to see what my enemy looked like in the light, but I couldn't find them. When daylight came, I realized the *monsters* I'd feared all night *didn't exist.*

The dogs were real, of course—but they were nothing like the creatures I had made them out to be. What I found instead were a few mangy strays that were thin, hungry, and scared. If they were anything like my dog, Sergeant Sweetcheeks, they were probably just terrified by the noise—running from fear and searching for peace of their own.

In the days that followed, we fed and named them. One became our border favorite: a white dog resembling Steve Martin's dog Shithead from the classic movie *The Jerk.* Some bored soldiers drew captain's bars on his fur, and he was forever known as "Captain Shithead." He slept beside us on the breach point, bringing joy where joy was uncommon.

After the darkness, when the light came, I found the opposite of what I feared. I found something to love.

THE MONSTERS WE INVENT

It's easy to laugh and see how absurd that is now—Private Brittain, scared of strays in the middle of combat—but fear in the dark does something to you. It exaggerates. It distorts. It makes puppies sound like wolves.

And when the sun rose? They weren't monsters. They were just survivors. They brought us joy, they lightened the mood, and they gave us something human to hold on to in an inhuman time.

What changed? *The light.*

Lesson: Fear doesn't need facts. It just needs darkness.

BEYOND SHOCK AND AWE: BLACKOUT OPERATIONS

You'd think one night like that would toughen me up—to prove I could handle the dark. It didn't. Shock and Awe may end, but fear doesn't always fade with it. The explosions stop. The cameras move on. But operating in the dark continues.

A few nights later, we were deeper in Iraq, escorting fuel north as the battle advanced toward Baghdad. The base we pulled into was on total blackout, where we had strict rules against using our headlights or any light at all. I'd practiced driving in the dark once before, in training, but this wasn't practice. This was real, with the enemy nearby and me with a convoy full of combustible fuel, depending on me. We slipped through the pitch-black maze wearing night vision goggles that warped everything in front of us. It was challenging to see anything clearly, especially depth or distance. The world looked like static green smoke, and my heart pounded. Every shadow felt like a cliff. Every turn felt like a trap, and yet, we kept moving—slowly, carefully, one cautious turn at a time.

Days later, we came back through that same camp in daylight. Without blackout rules or night vision goggles at play, what I saw made me laugh out loud. The narrow, dangerous path I'd imagined? It was a wide, flat, open road. A child could've driven it.

Perspective changes everything.

Darkness lies—not always through fear, but sometimes through distortion. What feels deadly at night can be simple by daylight. And when you're leading others through darkness—whether emotional, tactical, or spiritual—you have to remember it's not always as bad as it feels. It is in those moments when we must ensure we operate with facts, not fear. If we can't see clearly enough to see what is real, communicate what you see and lean on your people to help. And, even when it's challenging, remain calm and trust that when the light returns, so will your clarity about the situation at hand.

FROM COMBAT TO CRISIS

Those nights taught me something I've carried through war zones, locker rooms, hospitals, grief, cancer, and coaching: What feels monstrous, terrifying, and overwhelming in the dark is often just misunderstood in the light—distorted, magnified, or stripped of its true form.

And when I say *dark,* I don't just mean the absence of light. I mean fear. Numbness. Shame. Guilt. Uncertainty. The space between who we were and who we're becoming. The weight of leadership when the map isn't clear.

In those spaces, the mind plays tricks. We catastrophize. We isolate. We turn our feelings into facts as we tell ourselves stories that *feel* real—but aren't always true. We hear the growl of something unknown and brace for the bite, only to find later it was never as close—or as dangerous—as we thought.

I've felt that darkness in hospital rooms, waiting for news about someone I love. I felt it when my doctor said, "The cancer has spread to your lymph nodes." And I've felt it most fiercely in the mirror—staring into my own hollow eyes, asking myself, *How on earth am I supposed to lead others if I can't even get myself through this?*

And every time, the path forward has started the same way—by finding enough light to see what's true and enough courage to keep moving toward it.

LEADERSHIP LENS

Fear in the Dark

Fear in the dark bends perception. It stretches shadows into threats and turns unfamiliar sounds into danger.

Most of what unsettles us in moments like these isn't the threat itself; it's the distortion created when we can't see clearly.

Leadership isn't about eliminating fear. It's about bringing enough light to restore perspective.

When clarity returns, courage looks different. It isn't the absence of fear—it's the decision to keep moving once you can see what's actually in front of you.

But not all darkness is imagined. Some nights reveal real wounds—loss, trauma, harm—that don't disappear with daylight. Those moments require a different kind of leadership, one rooted not in reassurance but in care and repair.

This chapter is about the darkness that distorts. Later, we'll face the darkness that truly injures.

TACTICAL TAKEAWAY

When fear starts building stories louder than facts, pause. Ask yourself:

- What's *real* here? (Facts)
- What's *imagined*? (Feelings or thought spirals)

Write both down. Then act only on what's true.

CHAPTER 3

LIES IN THE DARK

ON MY SECOND deployment to Iraq, I was determined to journal. I fumbled the opportunity to capture the experience in 2003, so on my return trip, one of my first stops was a small shop that sold handmade journals.

I chose one with thick, textured pages and a leather cover embossed with a camel. A thin piece of string wound around the cover, tying it shut. I loved it because it was simple, rugged, and somehow felt sacred, as if it were something meant to hold adventures.

I began documenting the journey casually. And then, abruptly, one day, I stopped.

February 24, 2009, was the day I stopped writing in that journal. I had decided early in that deployment to record the experiences, people, and adventures that made that year memorable. I didn't know that one sentence would mark the end of it—and a change in me.

One of the last lines I ever wrote was quite telling for the trajectory of my life to follow: "I go numb, and I just want to go to work."

Here's how I got there: I was the battle desk noncommissioned officer (NCO) in the Battalion Tactical Operations Center (TOC), where I was responsible for tracking operations for nine military police companies that were running the police-primacy mission across northern Iraq.

A year earlier, a back surgery had grounded me and prevented me from the initial deployment I was supposed to go on. When I had healed enough to deploy, I was assigned to the tactical operations cell in our battalion operating in Tikrit instead of running patrols with my squad in Mosul. Watching my people go outside the wire—taking contact and enduring near-daily rocket and mortar attacks—while I sat in the safety of a cushioned chair in an air-conditioned office felt wrong, and it cut deep into my sense of identity as a leader. I was already recovering from being broken and aching to be with them, but I poured everything into the new role to serve every troop in the fight.

On February 24, a battle captain rushed into the TOC—eyes wide, voice sharp. "SSG Brittain! Find out who was hit in Mosul. The landowner says an MP was shot!"

Two companies worked that area—one of them contained my old platoon: the same group that held my best friends from my first deployment and the soldiers I had once led and still felt responsible for. These were *my people*, and I was terrified of the news I might hear.

My throat tightened as I called the 302nd TOC, and my old platoon sergeant answered. Relief washed over me at the familiar voice on the other end of the line. I had known him for six years, and we'd been through a lot together, but I had never heard his voice like it was in that moment—tight with concern. The only thing I could get out was "Was it us?"

"Yes, it's us. But, Britt, it's the 269th attached element. Not your guys," he said gently, like a big brother trying to steady me.

In the world of combat operations, that meant a platoon from another company out of Tennessee had been temporarily attached to ours from Texas to strengthen coverage in a rough sector. The 2008 surge had pushed violence out of most cities, but Mosul stayed messy—a place where the fight refused to die down. They were assigned to our battalion and attached to my people. So, while I didn't know the element that was hit, they were still family in the fight.

I would later learn that some very good friends were among the first to arrive for the medical evacuation. One of my best soldiers was in the gunner's turret, doing everything he could as they raced the wounded to the combat-support hospital. Knowing they were the ones facing this while I sat behind a desk hit harder than I can explain.

The words "not your guys" should have brought relief—and they did, for a literal moment—but the relief itself felt wrong. Because in combat, there's no such thing as *not your guys*.

As that realization sank in, his tone on the other end of the line shifted back to the noise around him. "We're in the middle of this! I'll call when I know more."

I stayed there, phone still in my hand, knowing the fight was happening far beyond my reach while I was trapped behind a desk with nowhere to send my effort to help.

I reported to our operations major and was told to stay on top of updates from the combat-support hospital (CSH). I called as often as the hospital staff would let me before reminding me—sometimes sharply—to let them work. Between calls, I updated everyone around me and stayed in contact with the 269th headquarters—the unit the attached platoon had been pulled from to support operations in Mosul. I promised to keep them informed of anything I learned. They trusted me to keep them updated on their soldier—the way I would have wanted someone to keep me informed if it were one of my closest friends.

The situation changed multiple times: *critical but stable, then stable, then critical again.* As it neared the late-night hours, a battle captain finally ordered me to get some rest. "Brittain, we need you tomorrow. You're no good if you stay here all night and don't sleep. We have a night crew for a reason. Go to bed. This is not a request."

I obeyed. I don't know how long my eyes were closed before—Knock. Knock. Knock. It was the night shift crew at my door. "I'm sorry, Staff Sergeant Brittain. He didn't make it. I know you wanted to be the one to call his people."

I laced my boots, wishing I'd never taken them off. When I slept, he had died. And in that silence, the words came for me. *If I had just been there . . .*

I didn't know it yet, but that sentence wasn't the truth. It was a lie grief told me, one that never actually existed outside my own mind. That thought felt like leadership, like ownership and accountability, but it wasn't. It was guilt disguised as honor, control dressed up as responsibility, and it planted itself like a seed, sending roots deep into my core for years to come.

EXPLORING THE EMOTION

Years later—long after I'd packed that camel-covered journal away in a box—I found it again. The leather was stiff, the string frayed. I untied it and opened to that final entry:

> *Journal—February 24, 2009*
> *"I start to cry, then I go numb, then I get mad, then I go numb and just want to work . . ."*

As mentioned, that was the moment my handwriting stopped, and, for a long time, so did I. We lost three more soldiers in my battalion that year. The violence and losses were made more intolerable by the complex, muddy realities of the war itself. With enough conviction to believe the counterinsurgency and transition policies we operated under were putting soldiers at risk, and enough humility to recognize that the goal of building a sovereign Iraq was far more complex than my tactical perspective, I grew frustrated, angry, and hopeless.

Not knowing how to process all of those emotions, I shut down. The version of me who wrote that line was already beginning to dim, trading grief for grind, pain for productivity. That year, I got a lot of work done on everything—*except myself.*

GRIEF LIES

Not only were the emotions of this deployment a challenge, but the thoughts that lingered impacted me deeply. *If I had just* became a pattern I didn't notice, growing deeper roots with each event after February 24. It showed up again when we had three more soldiers die in an explosively formed projectile (EFP) blast. It showed up when it didn't even make sense, when I had no control over a situation, when a rational person would never expect to impact life and death. It had an unhealthy habit of showing up in rooms it did not belong in:

When a student was killed in a drug raid: *If I had just gotten through to him.*

When a student died by suicide: *If I had just kept in touch with him better.*

When a family member went to prison: *If I had just understood her better and helped her through her addiction.*

Each version of that sentence told me I was in control of outcomes I never controlled. It let me trade helplessness for self-blame—and call it leadership. But guilt without truth isn't leadership. *It's a lie.* And lies repeated to ourselves become beliefs.

APOLOGIZING TO A TREE?

I came home from that deployment in 2009 with a Bronze Star I didn't feel like I deserved, while four soldiers from our battalion came home in caskets draped in flags.

At my first coming-home party, I drank too much. I remember choosing to sit alone in my friend's backyard, where I saw a tree with four large branches. For reasons I still can't fully explain, in my drunkenness, I decided it was *them*. It made no sense, but I was in a dark place that night, and alcohol didn't help.

I ended up on my knees, hugging that tree, sobbing and apologizing to the soldiers who I believed I had let die. My friends tried to help, but I was inconsolable. I wanted to be sad. I wanted to be alone with those we lost.

That's what unspoken grief does. It finds a stand-in for the words you can't yet say out loud: *My heart is broken, and I wish I could have changed the story.*

Sober and healthy, I know I had nothing to apologize for, and, yes, it's embarrassing to admit that I was apologizing to a tree. But that night, the false story was running the show: *It was my fault. If I had just . . . they'd still be alive.*

The truth is, I did my job to the best of my ability. I cared deeply. I carried what was mine—and what was never mine. The event hadn't broken me; the story I told myself about it had.

I don't tell this story because it makes sense or because I'm proud of it. I tell it because it's true, and because somewhere, someone may still be living under the weight of the same lie—even if they're not ready to hear this yet. Maybe it's time to put the *if I had just* down.

THE LIE UNMASKED

If I had just feels noble because it mimics accountability. But real accountability asks, *What can I learn? What can I fix so this doesn't happen again?* The lie shouts, *You failed.* The first invites growth. The second demands punishment. That's how guilt disguises itself as leadership. It convinces us we can control the uncontrollable, then condemns us when we can't. It tells us shame is proof we cared.

It isn't.

You can honor those you've lost without carrying their ending as your burden. You can lead fiercely and still remember you were never meant to rescue everyone.

TALK TO YOURSELF LIKE YOU WOULD A FRIEND

When guilt loops take over, ask yourself the following:

- How would I talk to my very best friend if they were in this situation?
- What judgment would I pass on them?
- If this were happening to someone I love, would I tell the story the same way—or would I change it?
- Am I as kind to myself as I am to others? If not—why?

Your leadership needs your *strength and ownership*. But it also deserves your *compassion*.

CLOSING REFLECTION

The year 2009 wasn't the first or last time I experienced loss or trauma. But coming home from that deployment was the first time I questioned if I was still the leader I was born to be. It was the first time I let something diminish the light I had to give this world.

Now I know: *We can't control trauma, but we can control the story we tell ourselves about it—and the wrong story will break us faster than the event itself.*

Should have and *could have* do not exist. I no longer carry *If I had just* as my story. I carry the truth: I was there. I did my best. I loved.

And that is enough.

LEADERSHIP LENS

Guilt has a convincing disguise. It dresses itself in leadership and calls the weight it hands you "responsibility."

It makes you believe you're being accountable when, in truth, you're punishing yourself for what you never controlled.

Every *if I had just* becomes friendly fire that we aim at ourselves.

Real accountability doesn't require shame—it requires honesty. Healing begins the moment you trade self-blame for truth and remember: Caring deeply never meant you were meant to carry everything.

TACTICAL TAKEAWAY

Four C's for Self-Correction[1]
When you hear that sentence rising—*If I had just . . .*—pause and run the drill:

1. *Catch it*: Notice your thought and say it out loud.
2. *Check it:* Is this fact, feeling, or fear?
3. *Correct it*: Rewrite the sentence as truth—what you actually did, gave, or learned.
4. *Choose it*: Take one small action forward rooted in compassion, not condemnation.

This is how you lead yourself back to steadiness—by replacing the story that breaks you with the one that builds you.[2]

Chapter 4

CARL—BETWEEN GRIEF AND GRIT

IT WAS A late night in January of 2015, and I was just about to fall asleep when my phone rang.

It was Bob. A dear friend. My boss. And one of the best high school football coaches Texas has ever seen. His voice was different. *Off*. The tone alone stopped me in my tracks before the words even landed.

"I can't get him out of my head. I just keep seeing him."

Two nights before this call, Carl, one of our senior student-athletes—a leader, a young father, a college-bound football player with dreams bigger than the block he grew up on—had just been murdered a few miles from our school by the "Trill Fam," a gang out of Fort Worth, Texas.

Bob had to identify his body and navigate the chaos that followed in his locker room. What follows isn't an attempt to explain Carl's death, but to explore what violent loss does to the leaders left standing afterward.

That phone call wasn't about strategy or logistics, and it wasn't initially about what to say to the team or even what came next. It was a raw, unfiltered call from one leader to a friend in the dead of night, sharing his struggle in the darkness: "This hurts. And I don't know what to do with it."

I told him, "I know."

But the moment the words left my mouth, my heart sank. Because the truth is—I didn't. I had been to war. I had seen violent death. But I didn't know *this*. I hadn't been the one to show up and identify the body of a player I loved like a son. I hadn't walked into a locker room full of young men and tried to lead them away from a never-ending gang war after their brother had just been gunned down in the street. I hadn't had to be a coach, a father figure, a leader, an untrained detective, and a funeral planner—all in the same breath.

So what the hell was I doing saying, "I know"?

I didn't know what he would face in the coming days as the murder made national headlines. But I *did* know something. I knew what it meant to oscillate between grief and grit in the aftermath of violent loss—to feel your heart ricochet between numbness and rage, love and hate, moral injury and despair.

I knew the exhaustion. I knew the loneliness. I knew the ache of watching others hurt while still caring deeply for them. And I knew what it was to carry all of that and still be called to keep leading and complete the mission.

I knew what might come next—the anger that crashes in like a wave, demanding the world *stop* and recognize the tragedy. But the world doesn't stop. The meetings go on. The expectations pile up. And people expect you to keep functioning through it all.

I knew the soul-level fatigue of showing up for others when your own heart is shattered—when the only thing holding you together is the weight of responsibility and the refusal to let anyone else fall apart.

But I also knew this: in the middle of all that pain, when a leader keeps showing up—not just for the job, but for the *people*—something sacred happens. The wounded leader begins to heal.[3] Not *after* the grief, but *inside* it. In the act of serving others, the heart starts to stitch itself back together.

And maybe that's why he called me.

THE MISSING PLAYBOOK

I don't know who else Bob reached out to that night. But I've had enough of these heavy moments in life to recognize the phenomenon. The moment when a leader is staring down a nightmare that no one prepared them for. And I know what most of us are looking for in that moment: *a playbook*. Some kind of step-by-step guide for how to lead people through unspeakable grief, unscripted chaos, and the kind of heartbreak that feels too big to carry.

But here's the truth: There *is* no playbook.

And maybe leadership, in these moments, isn't about answers at all. Maybe it's about presence. It's about being a safe place to land, a steady voice, a flicker of light. A person who can help bring some of the darkness into the open, where it can finally start to lose its grip, because when pain stays hidden, it grows heavier.

When it stays in the dark, it starts to distort. I've already shared this truth: We can make monsters out of puppies in the dark. So, imagine what kind of fears and levels of despair we can create out in the middle of *real* trauma.

This is why the call matters. Not to fix the pain. But to face it—together.

MORE THAN A GAME—THE DAY AFTER CARL'S DEATH

A day before the call from Bob, I had my own journey with my own team and my own locker room to navigate. But coaching in this space wasn't just about basketball; it was about leading through violent loss when the calendar doesn't stop and the world expects you to keep functioning anyway. It feels almost shallow to bring this story into the world, but maybe that's why it has to be told. Because this is the part of leadership no one prepares you for and no one talks about— the kind that lives in the quiet moments after tragedy, when you're expected to show up, carry others, and hold it all together, even when you're breaking.

The day after Carl's murder, Martin High School felt heavy. Grief and shock hung in the air. The hallways were quieter. Students cried between bells. One of my players found me, hugged me, and then collapsed into my arms—sobbing uncontrollably. She had just lost one of her best friends to gun violence, and there wasn't a damn thing I could do to change that.

And then the bell rang, and class went on. The harsh reality in life is that the world keeps moving, even when yours stops. I learned that inescapable truth as a young soldier coming home from war. Sitting in the quiet, feeling numb as I watched the news. Soldiers were dying in the Middle East, but on the screen, they weren't people with families or names; they were just a ticker of numbers scrolling by while the rest of the world just kept moving.

Now, I was watching that same quiet indifference inside a school in the town where I grew up. Some students were devastated while others barely registered the loss, unsure if they'd ever even crossed paths with the kid everyone was talking about. In a school of close to four thousand students, I suppose that can be expected, but it still felt wrong.

That night, we had a huge district game—the biggest of my coaching career up to that point. We were in a position to compete for the first district championship, facing our cross-town rival. But grief didn't care, and neither did the district calendar. Carl wasn't a player on my roster, but he was one of our own. He was part of our warrior family. Not only was he friends with my players, but also I saw him nearly every day outside my classroom, where he always offered a smile and a quick "Hey, Coach."

Our game tipped off at the exact same time as his candlelight vigil. While our community gathered to grieve and honor his life, my team played in a quiet gym across town. We played alone that night, even though we wanted to be at the vigil with the rest of our community. No one asked if we should pause the game in order to let my players join the vigil. Campus leaders were too busy dealing with the struggles for a whole campus, and I had never entertained what to do in a moment like that, so I never thought to ask.

No one teaches you what you should ask for or expect in those moments. We all wanted to play, and we wanted to win, but we were also all in pain. So, we hit the floor, gave everything we had, and lost to a strong and deserving opponent—one who would go on to win the district championship.

After the game, I told my girls I was proud of them and that I loved them. But I wasn't prepared for the locker room that followed. I wasn't ready to look teenage girls in the eye and see them carrying a similar grief to the one I had known in Iraq, and then try to talk about a basketball game in the same space.

When I got home, all of that emotion spilled out. I punched my wall, slid down it, and sobbed. I was embarrassed that I cared so much about a game and how unfair the timing felt. I was angry that Carl was killed and heartbroken that his son had lost his father. And I was devastated knowing that some of my players still walk streets where gangs and guns wait around corners.

Leadership in moments like that can feel cruel. You're expected to be the strong one and carry other people's grief, steady the ship, and show up like you're OK—even when you're not. You're supposed to remind your players that it's OK to not be OK and then somehow rally them to compete anyway. And when it doesn't end the way you hoped, you're supposed to smile, shake hands, and say, "It's just a game."

No one really trains a coach or leader on how to lead in the wake of trauma. How to be the adult in the room when your heart is shattering. How to keep the mission moving while you oscillate between grit and grief. How to teach kids to lose with grace when the loss is layered in pain that has nothing to do with a scoreboard. And yet, we lead. Even in those moments where everyone would understand if we chose to sit down, we still get up and continue the mission.

Because for many of us, it's not *just* a game or job. We've poured our time, energy, and hearts into building something that matters. We've asked our teams to sacrifice for each other, to buy in, to dream big, to chase something together.

So sure, technically, it's just a game. But if that's all it is, I wouldn't be the kind of coach I want to be. Because it's *always* more than a game. It's life. It's family. It's legacy. And that's what makes leadership sacred. You don't get to step back just because your heart is breaking. You lead anyway. You show up anyway. You carry the weight—even when it feels unbearable. You protect your team's light—even when yours is flickering. Because that's the paradox of leadership after loss. The game *matters*—and *it doesn't*.

The grief matters. The loss matters. The love matters. The effort, the showing up, the fight to keep moving—all of it matters. Leading through heartbreak means holding space for both: the ache of what's gone and the hope of what we still pursue.

It all matters—every bit of it. Because leadership amid loss lives in that sacred space between grief and grit, the messy intersection *where heartbreak meets courage.*

THE OSCILLATING FAN OF GRIEF AND GRIT

I've always liked oscillating fans—something about the way they work, the way they shift focus when needed, is something I've always appreciated. When I was a kid, I'd come in from playing in the Texas summer heat, snap the button up, and lock the fan in one place so it would hit me directly. I needed it to stay there—to cool me down and help me catch my breath. But once I'd cooled off, or someone else needed it, I'd release the button and let it swing, sharing the air with the rest of the room.

There are times in life when we have to lock it in and times when we have to let it swing somewhere else.

When a fan oscillates, it can't focus on the whole room at once. It lingers on one side, then shifts its attention to the other—cooling one space before returning to the next. That rhythm has always stayed with me.

There's a reason the oscillating fan has stuck with me as a metaphor. Grief doesn't move in a straight line. Neither does leadership after loss. One moment you're locked in on a mission—continuing your daily duties, planning the funeral, leading the team through the next practice. The next, you're doubled over with a grief you didn't see coming, wrecked by a memory or a silence that hits too hard.

That swing? It's not failure. It's *function*.

Psychologists Stroebe and Schut call it the *dual process model of coping with bereavement*[4]—a natural and necessary shift between *loss* and *restoration*. Between pain and forward motion. Between the heaviness of what was lost and the hope of what still needs to be done.

If there's one thing I've learned, it's that there is no perfect rhythm to this. Your oscillation won't look like anyone else's. You might see someone powering through work while you're breaking down, and assume they're stronger. Or maybe you're the one who looks composed while someone else crumbles—and you wonder what's wrong with you for feeling so numb.

Don't compare the swing you *feel* in yourself to the swing you *see* in others. You may only be witnessing one end of their fan. This isn't a competition. It's survival. There is *no one right way* to oscillate between grief and grit. It's a personal rhythm—sometimes daily, sometimes hourly—and it takes time to trust your own flow.

So if you're leading through trauma or loss, here's your reminder that it's OK to

- swing between feeling the loss and continuing the mission;
- coach the game (or mount up and continue mission);
- not coach the game (it's OK to say you need to sit this one out);
- need both and not know which one until you're in it;
- not feel like your best self all the time (in fact, it's human); or
- continue business as usual if that helps you heal and you need to process on your terms at your time.

And when you stop judging yourself for how you're navigating it—and stop assuming you know how others are navigating theirs—you can breathe again and focus on *your* needs. You can lead again. And eventually, you can heal inside the swing.

LEADERSHIP LENS

Grief doesn't ask for permission. It walks straight into the spaces leadership lives—the gym, the sideline, the conference table—and dares you to keep breathing while everyone looks to you for direction.

The weight isn't just sadness; it's responsibility in a room filled with loss.

Leadership in tragedy isn't about holding everyone together—it's about *remaining present* when nothing makes sense.

Grit isn't loud, and it's more than toughness. It's the perseverance that lives between breaking and becoming—steadiness under fire, the will to move forward with what's left.

TACTICAL TAKEAWAY

In full honesty, it feels inauthentic to offer a true "tactical takeaway" here—yet.

One day, after completing my dissertation and learning from others who've walked this same road, I plan to return to this space with more to give.

For now, this is what I know and have to offer the leader who is searching for tools: When the unthinkable happens, don't rush to fix the pain or find all the right words. *Presence is the first act of leadership after loss.*

You don't need a speech, a plan, or a perfect response. You just have to stay steady enough for others to know they're not alone.

In grief, *routine is the rope*. It's what people hold when everything else feels like it's falling apart. Small things—unlocking the gym, turning on the lights, greeting your team, showing up when it hurts—remind everyone the team still exists, even when a piece of it is gone.

Leaders can't erase pain, but they can hold space for healing—proving that love didn't leave when loss arrived.

CHAPTER 5

DISCONNECTION

S OME PERIODS IN life hit heavier than others, and nine months after Carl was killed, 2015 presented another challenge that hit my leadership light. You can be steady for everyone else and still be undone by a season you never saw coming. For me, one of those seasons came at the start of a new basketball season, when my friend Jane Ellen—"Mama Slagle" to all the players on my team—passed away after a long fight with cancer. Some parts of that story are still too sacred to speak, and maybe they always will be. But I can tell you this: It crushed my spirit in a way even war hadn't.

We held her funeral on my basketball court. It was a packed house in her favorite place. She had run the scorer's table for me for years, keeping the scorebook just a foot from my coaching chair during every high school game her daughter played, no matter what treatment struggles she faced while battling multiple myeloma. At times, she had to catch herself from cheering for—or shouting at—her all-time favorite player, number twenty-four. Her daughter, Emily.

The day of the funeral, that scorer's table became part of her memorial. We had "Mama Slagle" screened across the back of jersey number twenty-four, and everyone signed it as they came in. No one embodied our Warrior spirit more, and that was clear by the turnout.

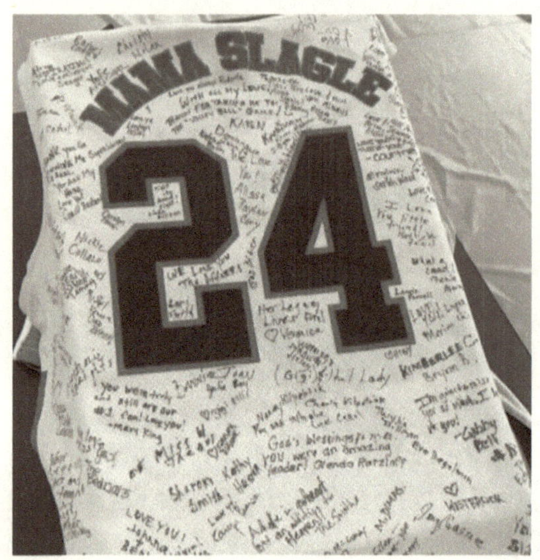

Signed jersey honoring the memory of Jane Ellen "Mama" Slagle

I stood on that court surrounded by my players, staff, community, and the young woman who had just lost her superwoman of a mother. Nothing about this loss felt fair or sat well in my spirit. Some things just shouldn't happen the way they do in this world, and this felt like one of them.

And in the middle of our basketball season, I was trying to oscillate between grief and grit—something I had lived before. But this time, the grit wouldn't come. Only grief. The fan swung all the way to one side and got stuck there.

In the months that followed, I couldn't find my footing. Some days, I didn't know if I could get off the couch. The fatigue wasn't just physical—it lived in my bones, my thoughts, my will.

That's when the disconnect started to surface. I missed more practices that season than I ever had when I was gone for three straight days right before New Year's. I flew to New Jersey to watch Slagle's team play and rode the bus back with them to Dartmouth because I wanted her to feel someone from home in the stands during the holidays. Honestly, I think I needed that trip more than she did, but it meant missing practice.

When I got back, I ran into a player I'd always felt close to. "I'm sorry I missed practice," I told her. "How did it go?"

She looked at me, shrugged, and—without a hint of malice—said, "You missed practice?"

High school kids can be brutally honest without even realizing it. Her words hit like a gut punch. It confirmed what I'd been afraid to admit: My body might have been there, but my presence hadn't. And if I could disappear for three days and no one noticed, what did that say about my leadership?

The fear crept in that I couldn't continue to lead like *this*. I began to believe that my team would be better off with a leader who was not broken. So, I did what many leaders do when the light flickers: I hid.

HIDING IN PLAIN SIGHT

I don't know exactly when it happened, but somewhere along the way, I stopped looking people in the eye. "How's it going?" became a drive-by question, and I never paused to connect. I made myself look hurried, too busy to stop. Sometimes I wouldn't even glance up, afraid of what eye contact might reveal.

I've always believed the saying that eyes are windows to the soul. You can feel so much in a person's eyes—love, their light, their humor, the sincerity of a smile, their kindness, or even their anger. I always made time to check in with others and connect, and I was taught to look people in the eye when I speak to them. But I couldn't risk that anymore. If I let someone look too closely, I was sure they'd see my truth: I was living a cold, dark, hollow existence.

So, I shut the blinds.

I stopped telling stories. Stopped sharing victories or struggles. I let laughter go quiet. I cut off the silly, playful parts of myself.

I was afraid they'd recognize that the light in me had gone dim. So, I hid in plain sight. I gave less of myself, thinking it was the only way to survive. But in giving less, I became less. And slowly, I shrank into the shadows of my own life.

From this time, I have come to believe that disconnection doesn't crash in—it creeps. One unnoticed moment, one missed glance, one unchallenged "I'm fine," stacked and compounded over time.

That's how light fades in leaders—it happens quietly while the work keeps getting done.

And underneath that slow crawl into normalcy? Fear. Fear of being seen. Fear of being judged. Fear that if people knew how tired or empty you really are, they'd lose faith in you. So you build walls and call them boundaries, and you stay busy and call it hustle.

But reconnection begins the same way disconnection did—quietly, one choice at a time.

One honest conversation.

One moment of eye contact.

One act of service.

One small display of gratitude.

And if you don't know where to start, start with the most powerful one: *serve someone.*

LEGACY LIGHT: THE JANE ELLEN SLAGLE SPECIAL OLYMPICS BASKETBALL TOURNAMENT

It took years before I could see it clearly, but service often became the place where my own healing quietly began. It's a truth I didn't recognize at first, but one that runs through this story. When Emily Slagle graduated and joined my coaching staff at Mansfield High School, we brought grit, joy, and laughter to the gym as a staff, but we also created something special in the community: *The Jane Ellen Slagle Special Olympics Basketball Camp and Tournament.*

Every season, we host athletes with special needs from across our district. Our first camp welcomed sixty-five Special Olympians ranging in age from eight to fifty-five, and we continue to grow each year. Jane Ellen taught special education and coached special needs athletes for more than thirty years before she passed, so this event feels like carrying her heartbeat forward.

What began as a way to honor her has become a living legacy that reconnects an entire community. As the gym fills with laughter, high-fives, growth, and gratitude, I can't help but think this is exactly the kind of space Jane Ellen spent her life creating for others. That kind of service has a way of expanding what you think you can carry and filling parts you thought were empty. Perhaps that is how Jane Ellen carried so much and still gave so much.

Final huddle at the First Annual JES MISD Special Olympics Basketball Camp

LEADERSHIP LENS

Presence over Performance

You don't need to be perfect. You need to be present.

Leadership isn't measured by never being broken. It's revealed in showing up anyway.

When you hide yourself, disconnection grows. Reconnection begins the moment you let yourself be seen again.

TACTICAL TAKEAWAY

Reconnect Before You Repair

If you feel distant, tired, or disconnected, it doesn't mean you are broken. It means grief, pain, and struggle have made it feel safer to hide.

You can't worry or shame yourself back into connection. You have to lean into it.

Start Small

- Reconnect with yourself.
- Make space for your own thoughts and healthy habits.
- Make eye contact.
- Offer a smile, handshake, or a high-five: Positive touch builds connection.
- Share one honest thought, feeling, or struggle with someone you trust.

Don't wait to feel ready to act. Small actions are what bring connection back.

Reconnection doesn't happen all at once. It happens one small choice at a time.

PART II

THE LIGHT

*Awareness of the dark
doesn't get you out of it.
You need enough light to see
what you're actually facing.
From there, you can begin to move
forward toward the fight.*

CHAPTER 6:

THE BULLET, THE BIAS, AND THE BATTLE WITHIN

I AM AN OPTIMIST trained for war.

That reality tends to surprise people. At work, it's not uncommon for me to be introduced as "the most enthusiastic person." In front of a crowd—pep rallies or faculty meetings—my colleagues invite me up to connect with an inspiring message and offer positive energy. When they do, they often introduce me with words like most optimistic, most encouraging, most joyful.

That reputation didn't come out of nowhere. My team at work recently watched me walk through a cancer battle with a smile on my face and the words relentlessly optimistic stamped across my T-shirt. They saw all of it. So when they describe me that way now, it's personal to them—and I genuinely appreciate it.

Beyond that season, optimism has always been part of how I move through the world. I'm naturally kind, empathetic, and forgiving. I tend to see the best in people, sometimes to a fault. I high-five coworkers, initiate interactions with a smile, say hello to strangers, and hold the door open for others whenever I can. I'm drawn to good energy, and I try to contribute to it in the world.

But here's the part people don't easily see: Alongside that optimism lives a mind trained to scan for danger. In combat, I was taught to always look for what could go wrong first. That negativity bias once served me well because it helped me identify threats and keep people alive. Long after the war ended, that same instinct followed me home; what once protected me eventually almost cost me everything.

HOW WAR TRAINED MY EYES

We all have a natural tendency to scan for threats. It is commonly discussed as a phenomenon of neuroscience:[5] our brains are hardwired to help us survive. Early humans stayed alive by spotting a lion in the brush and reacting fast. There is still a valuable place for that ability in our lives.

That wiring saved my life when I was twenty years old and at war for the first time. Some of it came naturally, and some of it was taught—like the time SSG Monte Mills chewed me out for driving over a pile of trash that could have been an improvised explosive device (IED). And some of it was pure instinct—like scanning my sector and locking my sights on to a person, object, or situation as a threat, not because I wanted to hurt anyone, but because I had to be ready to take care of my people.

As a young adult, I spent 366 days at war and turned twenty-one in a combat zone. Somewhere in that year, my brain leaned hard into a powerful capacity—the ability to both love people while appreciating life and simultaneously scan for things that wanted to kill me. In that space, it wasn't a contradiction. It was survival.

That capacity exists in all of us. War just turned it all the way up in me.

Here's what that looked like:

I could roll into a town, smile, and wave at the kids in Safwan who danced when they saw us coming. I genuinely enjoyed them. But in a split second, if something felt off—if the kids weren't out, if a new face appeared, if the energy shifted—I'd drop the smile, lower my profile, narrow my eyes, and prepare for the worst.

There were days that tested that switch. I'd been in that same town just hours earlier, connecting with good people, feeling joy, and dancing like a goofball with my favorite kids. Then, almost without warning, hours later, we rolled into an ambush point. In a split second, I went from clear road to driving over a makeshift roadblock with car bumpers and bricks piling up at a narrow pass in the road. This is an immediate signal in combat: *Someone is trying to kill me right now.*

As I floored the gas, I went into full Ninja Turtle mode—tightening into my "shell," helmet pressed hard against my flak vest while I braced for a blast. As I busted through the early-stage roadblock at full throttle, nothing happened. I slid out of my makeshift turtle shell and looked at SSG Mills. No words were needed. Just a shared glance that said, *Holy shit. That was almost bad.*

We made it through the kill zone and crossed back into Kuwait with the nearly fifty fuel tankers we were escorting behind us. Unfortunately, the Marine convoy behind us wasn't as lucky. They were ambushed with gunfire at the same blockaded choke point.

The threat was real, and the margin between luck and loss had never felt thinner.

In moments like that, I could forget every good thing about those people and that town—and I *had to.* That swing from joyful connection to extreme hypervigilance wasn't just helpful; it was life or death. This was a great combat skill. The problem came later.

When I came home, I didn't always know how—or where—to set that skill down. Instead of seeing all of the good things I could enjoy around me, I started seeing threats first. In Iraq, that wiring kept me alive. At home, it kept me braced for impact in rooms where there was no actual danger.

THE BULLET IN MY POCKET

There was more than just threat spotting going on in my brain that year. I brought another challenge home that I fully intended to leave in combat, and it started with an inside joke with the "the Tough Guys." We were four female soldiers in a male-dominated military police unit—combat-ready and determined to survive Iraq with our dignity intact, no matter what war threw our way. The first time we vocalized what that might look like came in the aftermath of a significant combat event during the early portion of the war.

On March 23, 2003, Private First Class Jessica Lynch, a supply clerk with the 507th Maintenance Company, was captured near Nasiriyah, Iraq, after her convoy was ambushed. Lynch was seriously injured when her Humvee came under fire and crashed during the ambush. I was told it made national news, but we lived it as her unit was attacked in our area of operations.

Word around the battlefield was that one of our company elements had escorted her convoy north along Main Supply Route (MSR) Tampa earlier that day. After dropping them at a camp, our military police company element turned back south for another escort mission. Without a security escort, her convoy continued on alone toward their next objective—where they were ambushed.

The rumors that followed were brutal—some real, some exaggerated or misinformed. Regardless, the detailed story we received hit hard: weapons malfunctioning due to the sand, ammunition running out, overpowering enemy forces, and finally, capture, torture, and rape.

For the Tough Guys, our hearts sank. We'd already heard that female soldiers were considered more "valuable" to the enemy because our capture would carry propaganda weight and change how America felt about the war. The thought of daughters and wives being killed, captured, or raped went far beyond the normal rules of combat.

We made a pact: *No. F—ing. Way.*

Each of us took a single bullet from our nine-millimeter magazines and tucked it into the left pocket of our combat uniforms—nearest our hearts. A backup plan. A line in the sand. A refusal to surrender our bodies to be raped by the enemy if it came to that.

We turned the terror into humor because that's how we coped. We started calling the bullet in our pocket "Barney Fife," the fictional deputy sheriff of Mayberry on *The Andy Griffith Show,* who wasn't allowed to carry ammo in his weapon. However, he always kept one bullet in his chest pocket *just in case*. We'd pat the lone bullet in our pockets like we were doing a uniform inspection and exchange a wordless nod and a giggle. Humor was the only thing that could make such a messed-up reality palatable. But that nod and giggle clearly meant *I've got mine. Do you have yours?*

We laughed, but we meant it. That bullet represented control in a world where very little felt within our control. It made us feel powerful in response to fear. Prepared. In charge of our own fate. Twenty years later, I still won't judge that choice. In that moment, it wasn't surrender—it was deciding what stories would make it home to our families and what part of ourselves we were willing to give someone else. But as a leader, I'd mentor young Private Brittain differently. I'd point her toward resilient leaders who endured similar horrors and kept fighting. I'd tell her about General Rhonda Cornum, who survived capture in the first Gulf War and later helped shape the Army's Master Resilience Training program with Dr. Martin Seligman.[6]

What I know now that Private Brittain didn't? That decision planted a dangerous seed.

If the fight wasn't on my terms, I could end it.

And that seed didn't stay in Iraq. It took root and came home with me.

THE GLOCK ON THE PATIO

In 2009, after losing four soldiers at war and drowning in the *if I had just . . .* guilt, I remember the moment the bullet in my pocket became the gun in my mouth.

I sat alone on my patio, picked up my .45-caliber Glock and put it between my teeth.

I thought through how I would do it. I considered whether I should. Then I put it away—telling myself it was there if I needed it. And I told no one for nearly a decade.

That wasn't just war catching up with me. It was my need for control—an old, combat-tested exit strategy fueled by negativity bias—showing up again when I didn't like the hand I'd been dealt. If the threat was a fight I didn't want to face, I believed it was mine to end.

THREAT OR JOY

Not too long ago, I heard Dr. Martha Beck talk about how our brains are wired to focus on threats instead of joy. In her book *Beyond Anxiety*, she uses an image that landed hard for me: Negativity bias is like being in a room filled with a thousand puppies and one cobra.[7]

I don't remember her exact words, but I remember the feeling. A space overflowing with joy, laughter, and goodness—and right in the middle, one threat pulling all my attention away. Where does my focus go? Away from the puppies I love and straight to the cobra that is threatening me. Of course it does; that's survival wiring.

In war, that instinct kept me alive. In leadership, it can smother your fire. Once your brain is trained to scan for danger, it doesn't always know when to stand down. Many of the things we perceive as threats in everyday life are completely *incapable of harming us*.

It's frustrating to realize how much time I gave to things that held no real power over me. That wasn't a cobra. That was negativity. But when I handed it my attention, it stole my focus from the things that actually mattered.

I could have fifty athletes who loved me and a hundred students thriving—and still fixate on one critic. A bad attitude, judgment, criticism, or my own false stories became a cobra. I wrapped it around my spirit and let it squeeze. Something harmless became harmful because I gave it power.

When that negativity bias paired with my old exit-strategy mindset, that cobra didn't just steal my focus; it stole my fight. These patterns were connected: negativity bias, old thought habits, quitting—whatever form it took. When all you can see is the threat, you stop fully showing up. You lead smaller. You risk less. You trade purpose for protection.

And before you know it, negativity bias doesn't just shrink your life—it shrinks your leadership and steals your focus.

FIGHTING BACK

I'm still an optimist—not because I've lived an easy life but because I've learned the hard way that if I don't fight for my light, the illusion of a threat will win. This isn't about pretending everything's fine; it's about refusing to hand over my fight to a threat that isn't even real.

Sometimes our fears are simply things we cannot see clearly yet. The shadow that felt dangerous? Turns out it was simply unfamiliar. *Negativity bias will try to convince you that every unknown shape is an enemy. But the more you turn on the light, the more you realize half the things you feared were never coming for you in the first place.*

I'm not saying no threats are real—some absolutely are. But I've wasted too many days and too much energy fighting the wrong ones. And every time I gave them my focus, my real work, my real joy, and my real purpose suffered.

Here's what I know: The habits that once kept me alive in combat can't take me where thriving begins in normal life. Every day, I get to decide what's worth my energy—and what I'll walk past without a second glance. And so do you.

No critic, no threat, no memory is worth keeping a bullet in my pocket ever again.

Because my fight now is for the light, not against the dark.

LEADERSHIP LENS

The Fight After the Fight

What once kept you alive can quietly start stealing your life. Leaders shaped by threat often mistake vigilance for wisdom and control for strength. But survival mode isn't meant to be permanent. When the war lives on in our thoughts, control feels like safety—and quitting starts to look like peace. Both are lies. Don't let imagined threats cost you real joy.

TACTICAL TAKEAWAY

Name the Threat

When your body tightens or your mind starts scanning, pause and name what you're reacting to. Is it danger—or discomfort?

Interrupt the Exit

Notice your default move when you feel exposed: pulling back, over-controlling, numbing out, or quietly quitting. Don't judge it—just don't obey.

Choose Presence over Protection

Stay in the conversation. Stay in the moment. Stay with people who matter. Connection is safer than control. Ask one simple question: Is this something *that can harm me—or something that's just uncomfortable?*

Discomfort calls for courage. Danger calls for defense.

Knowing the difference keeps you in the fight that matters.

CHAPTER 7

REORIENT YOUR MAP

WHEN THE PATH disappears, you have to use your compass. There's a moment in many hard seasons when you realize *I don't know where I am anymore. I don't know where I am going. And I don't know how to get back.*

Sometimes it's after trauma. Sometimes it's in the middle of a leadership role you used to love that just isn't filling your purpose tank. Sometimes it's when everything around you has shaken up and you can't see it clearly anymore. Maybe it's just waking up and realizing you don't recognize yourself. It can be disorienting. And in my life, the only way I've ever found to get back on track is the same way I did in the Army when we got lost on a mission:

You reorient.

You don't panic. You don't sprint in the wrong direction.

You stop. You check your map. You find something solid. And you reorient yourself to make sure you are headed in the right direction.

LOST IN THE DESERT

Before the initial invasion of Iraq, as we were staging for combat, I was a young soldier conducting a security escort mission of buses full of soldiers to small forward operating bases scattered across the Kuwaiti desert. My team leader trusted me to navigate and diligently familiarize myself with the route and map overlays before we set out. Our military police unit was running missions without the technology that was starting to become available for missions during that time. For the first six months of combat, we did all operations with nothing but a paper map, a compass, and a whole lot of *figure-it-out.*

We left the main supply route and headed into alternate routes where smaller camps were scattered—no road signs, no clear landmarks, just windblown terrain that shifted faster than we could read it. The path ahead didn't look like anything we'd studied or could make much sense of on our map. And, when you're responsible for people's lives, you can't stop and wait for rescue or directions. You have three choices:

- Freeze and fail in your mission.
- Push forward blindly, even if you are going the wrong way.
- Or pause, reorient, and get your bearings.

We chose the third.

We stopped the convoy, and I climbed onto the hood of my Humvee, scanning the horizon for any familiar landmarks, hoping to see some sort of distant camp or tents. My team leader and I checked our compass against the map and compared it to our starting point—verifying at least that they pointed in the same direction. A map can guide you when you have roads to follow, but in the windswept desert, when nothing familiar is present, a road map will not do. You need a compass to guide you. Once we used our compass to reorient our map, we could adjust our route with more confidence. Slowly, we found our way.

Mission complete.

That day taught me something I've carried into every other battlefield, military or otherwise. When the road disappears, the map is secondary. So often in life, people ask for a road map or a playbook on how to "handle the heavy," or navigate all of the adversity and crises they may face. But what I know is that when you are in unfamiliar territory, and the path is not clear, only a compass can point you true.[8]

In life, my compass is my presence in this world. It is how I show up and where I am going. That is determined by my *attitude and values.*

- *The needle is my attitude.* It shifts day to day, sometimes steady, sometimes distortion causes it to spin, but it is my job to be aware of where it is pointing and if I am allowing it to lead me in the right direction.
- *The directions are my values.* They are the fixed points that never change.

If I'm ungrateful, stuck in victim mode, selfish, petty, or entitled, my needle spins. I can't even begin to choose the right path. But when my attitude is set toward gratitude, courage, and service before self—and my values are fixed—I can reorient and find my way with any map life hands me.

Once the compass is true, the path starts to make sense again.

WHEN MY COMPASS SAVED ME

There was a season at work where everything flipped overnight.

Every leader I served under changed—mentors gone, stability gone, and the path I thought I was on suddenly blurred, all in the middle of a foggy fight with cancer. I went from feeling protected under an umbrella of leadership I trusted completely to standing out in the open in a storm in one of my most vulnerable seasons.

The uncertainty and unfamiliarity of my situation bled into everything. My attitude slipped, and although I am not proud to say it, my gratitude was the first thing to go. I found myself sliding back into that old negativity bias, my fuse growing shorter by the day. I caught myself staring at the "press here to resign" button on my computer screen more times than I'd like to admit.

Here's the thing—when the needle of my attitude spins, I can't align with my values, so I am left directionless. True clarity is gone, and the steps I start taking in anger, frustration, or out of sheer spite may not actually take me anywhere I am trying to go.

Thankfully, I stopped and went back to what I knew was solid. My compass points remain unchanged: I knew my most deeply held values and my commitment to aligning my thoughts, actions, and decisions with them.

I asked myself: *If I align my path to these values, what does the next step look like?*

It didn't give me the whole map back—I still needed to learn how to navigate the new terrain. But it gave me something more important—direction I could trust myself to travel in as I carved my own path. And when the terrain is chaotic, trusting your direction is everything.

YOUR ATTITUDE

This isn't about toxic positivity. It's about deliberately choosing:

- Gratitude over cynicism
- Courage over fear
- Service before self
- Optimism over pessimism
- Hope over despair
- Strengths over struggles
- Belief over doubt
- Encouragement over discouragement

Your attitude points you toward possibility instead of paralysis. And once you're pointed in the right direction, even the smallest step is progress.

DISTORTED DIRECTION

I noted earlier that when we were lost in the desert, I *stood on top of my Humvee* to get a usable compass reading. Here's why: Inside that walled-up hunk of steel and comms equipment, the needle spun with interference. The distortion may have even been part of why we got off course in the first place. But once SSG Mills and I climbed out and rose above the clutter as we looked for known points, the compass steadied, and we could move forward.

A compass follows earth's magnetic field, but large metal objects and electronics distort it. Life works the same way. We live in a world of clutter, and sometimes you have to step away from interference to read your own internal compass.

Here's what that clutter often looks like:

- *Energy contagion.*[9] Psychologists Elaine Hatfield and colleagues found that emotions spread between people automatically—through facial expressions, tone, and body language—often before we even realize it. One person's emotional state can infect an entire group in seconds.
- *Mob mentality.*[10] Psychologist Philip Zimbardo's research on deindividuation showed how people can lose their sense of self in a crowd. When identity blurs, conscience fades. Noise replaces reason, and we drift wherever the loudest voice is pulling—even when it's the wrong way.
- *Conformity.*[11] Social psychologist Solomon Asch's 1951 experiment showed that people often follow the crowd even when the crowd is clearly wrong. When placed in a group that unanimously gave

incorrect answers to an obvious question, more than a third of participants conformed at least once. Conforming is easy—it costs nothing and risks nothing. But if you want to keep your compass steady, you can't determine your direction based on the noise around you.

Thinking back to my professional shake-up, not only was I struggling, but also many around me were unsettled and feeling the same way as they navigated the same new situation. I let uneasy energy drown out my own bearings. I thought I was heading north—doing the right thing—but in reality, I was drifting south because my compass was cluttered with interference.

CLEARING THE CLUTTER

- *Make space for your own thoughts first.* In a world of social media, if our first (and sometimes only) step each day is to take in the thoughts and opinions of others, when do we have time to sort through our own?
- *Close the vents.* Every vent leaks into other rooms. Sharing and processing emotions with a trusted foxhole friend is one thing. Complaining or gossiping about matters surrounding your mission and other members of your team is another. What you vent in one room spreads, poisoning relationships and shaping the attitudes of those around you.
- *Go direct.* Talk to the person, not the crowd.
- *Name your feelings.* Ask, "What am I feeling—and why?"
- *Reflect with purpose.* Ask, "What do I want? What's within my control? How do I get there?"
- *Own your energy.* You are responsible for the energy you bring into your team, your organization, and your relationships.
- *Ground in gratitude.* Negativity is easy—our brains are wired to find threats. Gratitude clears the clutter and steadies your compass on what actually serves you.

VALUES ARE YOUR FIXED POINTS

If my attitude is the needle, my values are the direction it's trying to lock on to. The needle can wobble in clutter, but north never moves. Values are the constants. They don't shift with circumstances, bosses, events, or seasons of life. They are the fixed points that give me direction when the map no longer makes sense.

Here's how to keep them steady in a world full of interference:

- *Practice self-awareness.* You can't command yourself if you don't know yourself. Be honest about what actually matters to you.
- *Let your calendar tell the truth.* What you consistently make room for is already shaping your direction.
- *Check your priorities.* When pressure hits, notice what you protect first—people or processes. That moment reveals your true priorities.
- *Live with integrity.* Your commitments, your energy, and your daily habits should point in the same direction as your stated values—or the words don't mean much.

Values aren't just words on a wall or a slide in a presentation. They're the fixed points that keep your direction clear. When your attitude aligns with your values, your compass is primed to guide you in the right direction.

CREATING YOUR VALUES

The more your values matter to you and the more you reflect on them, the more they can lead you. My true north is that I am a vessel for God, and I want to do all things in alignment with what serves His people. Beyond that, I have many values that guide me, but I like to think the best values are simple and memorable. The ones I can call on in moments of complexity. Those are the ones you keep, and those are the ones you stack. I have been stacking values that matter to me my entire life:

- My first basketball coach gave me a values card in the eighth grade. On the back of a small team card, it simply said "1-2-3." He told us: *God, Family, Self. If you keep those in the right order, you'll have your life in order.* I knew he was right, and I never forgot it.
- The United States Army gave me another set when I was nineteen: *LDRSHIP.*[12] *Loyalty. Duty. Respect. Selfless Service. Honor. Integrity. Personal Courage.* Those seven letters became my backbone.
- As a coach, I've given my team our TIGERS values: *Toughness, Integrity, Gratitude, Enthusiasm, Respect, Service.* To expect these from my team, I must first model them in everything I do.

TIGERS Value Tags

- As a campus leader, I built a personal set of values for myself in regard to interactions and influence with the coaches and students I serve—I aim to star in my ROLE: *Resilience. Optimism. Leadership. Empathy.* Those words remind me of how I want to show up every day from the seat I am in.

When I lay them out like this, it might seem like a lot of values to keep up with, and, yes, I have more to add to the list, but none of these were built overnight—they were laid over time, brick by brick, each from a season that required it. Over the years, they settled into place, becoming part of the structure that steadies me. I don't recite them every morning or carry a list in my pocket. They're already built into the walls of my life because I remember choosing to pick them up.

When life applies pressure, I don't have to scramble for direction, and I already know what I want to come out when I'm squeezed. That's what values are for: not clutter but construction. They don't compete; they collaborate. Together, they form the framework that holds you steady when the storm hits.

So how do you create your own values?

Here are three quick ways:

- *Look back.* What words or lessons were given to you that still matter to you?
- *Look in.* What do you want people to know you stand for when you walk into the room?
- *Look forward.* What kind of leader do you want to become—and what values will get you there?

Once you've named them, write them down—not to recite every day, but to remember what matters. The act of writing helps you see what's already guiding you and what might need to be strengthened. Over time, those values stop being a list to learn, and they simply start becoming part of you.

As you navigate seasons of life and changing roles, you may find periods that require a new focus. So, when your foundation is full, narrow your aim to now. Focus on the values that serve your current role and guide your actions in this season of life. Keep them in sight as reminders while you navigate unfamiliar terrain. Eventually, they'll move from paper to practice—from something you write down to something that *guides you.*

If you let them, your inner compass will do what maps and manuals cannot: It will point you in a direction you can always trust.

LEADERSHIP LENS

Clarity Before Speed

Reorienting doesn't mean you've failed—it means you're paying attention.

You don't have to be failing to be off course. Even the best leaders drift.

The more chaotic the terrain, the more often you pause, check your bearings, and adjust.

The first step back isn't always motion—it's reflection. Clarity before speed.

Leaders who last the longest aren't the ones who never veer; they're the ones who stop, reorient, and move with purpose.

TACTICAL TAKEAWAY

Conduct a Tactical Halt

- *Pause.* Don't rush through confusion—take a tactical halt and get your bearings.
- *Ask.* Where am I—mentally, emotionally, and spiritually—right now?
- *Align.* Check your compass: Are your attitude and values leading your direction?
- *Move.* When the confusion clears, move with purpose toward what matters most.
- *Maps change. The compass doesn't.*

Sometimes the smartest thing a leader can do is pause and reflect long enough to make sure the next step is the right one. In those moments, when the path disappears, use your compass—your values—to find true direction again.

CHAPTER 8

NAVIGATING SPAGHETTI JUNCTION— THE WHOLENESS BLUEPRINT

DURING THE FIRST days of the war in Iraq, we ran a route reconnaissance mission up to a place the British troops called Spaghetti Junction—or, in my terrible British accent: *Spa-geh-EE Junk-shun, gov'nah.* It sat near the southern border in Safwan, a tangle of intersecting highways where convoys, tanks, and supply trucks wove through each other without a single stoplight. Spaghetti Junction was chaos that somehow worked. If you stayed sharp, you could glide right through. Lose focus for a second, and you'd find yourself facing the wrong way.

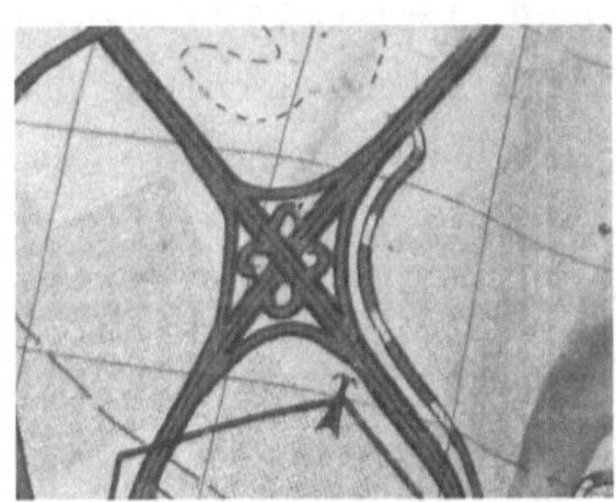

Spaghetti Junction—Safwan, Iraq

Decades later, when I began studying how high school coaches lead teams through violent loss, that junction came back to me. Leadership under stress feels exactly like that—fast, tangled, no clean intersections providing guidance on when to stop. It's a spaghetti junction—grief merging with mission, care weaving through exhaustion, moral injury crossing into responsibility—all of it moving at once, with no red lights. I've driven that road in more ways than one, and I know how easy it is to get lost on it. My first confusing twist was when moral injury collided with integrity and excuses. Without a stop sign at the intersection of leadership and trauma, it was easy to take the wrong path and go in a direction I did not want to travel.

INTEGRITY REBUILT

Understanding integrity better helped me navigate this road. In the Army, integrity meant one thing: Do what's right—legally and morally. War complicated that definition. I came home with memories and stories that made me question what was right in the world. I realized that right and wrong can feel simple in a handbook, but complex in a human heart.

War leaves marks you don't always recognize right away. Moral injury is a fracture in the part of you that once believed you were doing the right thing—and you struggle to look in the mirror with pride once you feel this internal conflict. When I came home, I wasn't just carrying wounds I could name. I was carrying invisible ones that I didn't have language for. And in that gap, something else crept in—excuses, self-doubt, and shame. When I was spinning, my actions, words, and values did not always line up.

For a while, I believed I'd lost my integrity altogether. And the way we talked about integrity in my world, once you lose it, that's it: You either have it or you don't. And if that is true, then why would I even try to fix the rest of my mess?

That belief let me live comfortably in the cracks with a cloud of self-judgment over my head. I thought I was broken beyond repair, so I stopped trying to fix much. I believed in forgiveness, of course. But integrity sat differently on my heart. One is about grace. Another is about being a good person I could be proud of. Thankfully, at some point, I heard a new definition of integrity, and I found it transformative as I considered it deeply.

In *Webster's* dictionary, you'll find integrity defined, in part, as "the quality or state of being complete or undivided"—whole. [13] Completeness means the necessary parts are present and aligned. That's what we know as structural integrity. When parts are missing or broken, it is incomplete—lacking *integrity*.

Moral injury, which I will dive deeper into later, made me feel like I'd lost my integrity *for good*.[14] I was cracked wide open—broken, incomplete—and I believed that meant I couldn't be whole again. But when the new definition of integrity—being whole and complete—took root in me, it reshaped how I understood myself and what it means to stay intact.

It's different from the blessing of forgiveness and finding healing. It's about holding on to *integrity in action*.

I now understand that integrity is not something I simply have or do not have. *It is something I protect. Something I maintain. Something I repair.*

Even in brokenness. I can move forward into integrity by repairing, maintaining, and protecting it. For the first time, I realized integrity wasn't about being spotless. It was about being *whole*.

Wholeness meant I could be a good person with *scars and stories*. I could carry moral injury, guilt, or failure—and still rebuild. It meant I wasn't doomed by the things I couldn't change or all of the breaks I let happen in the struggle. It also meant I was *responsible for repairing the parts I could.*

That mindset shifted everything, and this is the image that drove it all home for me:

Think of a bicycle wheel that has all of its components that make it *whole* and *a complete wheel*. It has many parts that make up its structural integrity, and they are all critical in supporting the ability of the wheel to carry weight without breaking under pressure. When every spoke is tight and strong and the tire is full, it rolls smoothly, even over rough ground. But let one spoke crack and leave it unrepaired—the pressure shifts. With one broken spoke, other spokes start to bend under new pressures. Then the rim wobbles. Eventually, the whole thing collapses.

That's how I have come to view integrity. It's not a thing you either have, or you don't; rather, it's all the healthy and strong parts working together that keep you whole and functioning well without breaking down. Along your journey, you must protect, check, and repair it, because even small breaks can cause major collapse over time. And the rougher the road, the more checks and repairs required.

MORAL INJURY AND LEADERSHIP

I was a young soldier in southern Iraq, stationed near Nasiriya with a small military police unit.

That's where I met the Bedour tribe, Bedouin people who had almost nothing but gave everything. Their kindness was simple, unshakable, and pure. We'd stop by after missions to check on them, help patch up small injuries, and enjoy their company over a cup of chai made with water dipped straight from the Euphrates River.

They didn't have much—a tent made of scrap material, a few blankets, some animals they raised—but they made you feel like you were home. In a world where everything felt dangerous, those moments felt peaceful, sacred, loving, and special. But one day, everything changed.

I still remember the boom felt down the road on November 12, 2003. The Italian base was hit with a suicide car bomb. Seventeen Italian soldiers were killed, and with the civilian toll, close to thirty died in a single blast. There was much to be learned about that bombing in the days that followed, but I didn't expect to hear about it from my Bedouin friends.

Brittain and Basim (Bedour Tribe)—Iraq, 2003

Brittain (left) and "Dot" Hardwick (right) with Bedour women

Father Tollock and daughters with Brittain

Days passed, and we finally had free time to go visit. But when we pulled in, they weren't the same smiling and enthusiastic crew that normally greeted us. Their eyes carried something I hadn't seen before—fear.

They begged for an interpreter who had visited with us before. When we returned with one, my friend Tollock told us insurgents had come, demanding their help with an attack. The Bedour tribe said no, and they had been desperate to see us again to tell us what was going on.

The insurgents told them they would be back, and next time they would demand that they go with them. They were told that if they did not go with the insurgents, the insurgents would kill them all. Our friendship had made them targets. These people had no enemies and wanted nothing to do with war, yet they still had violence pushed upon them. They wanted protection, training, weapons—anything that could help fight back against the threat they now faced.

And I had nothing to give.

I'll never forget the look in their eyes. That kind of fear doesn't need translation.

We checked on them frequently in the months that followed, but when we told them we were returning home, they desperately wanted to come with us. They thought everyone in America was safe and free, and they wanted to experience that.

Without a translator riding with us on most visits, communication was tricky, but we got creative. For example, when we discussed time, we used one of the few English words they knew: *Tomorrow*. So if I were trying to say something was three days away, we would raise three fingers, point, and say, "Tomorrow, tomorrow, tomorrow." On our final goodbye, I only had two words. One Arabic and one English. I said softly, "*La* tomorrow."

No tomorrow.

Their faces fell. They gave me a hug, and it was the last time I ever saw them.

Not long after we left, I heard about major attacks in the area. What we experienced in 2003–2004 was mild in comparison to the many years of violence that followed. For years, I watched ISIS tear through the country, the violence unfolding nightly on my news screen, and every news story made me worry about them.

To this day, I don't know who survived, but I've prayed for them ever since. It took me decades to realize that stories like these from war are where some of my cracks began—not from doing something wrong but from witnessing or being part of something I couldn't make right. I know I was proud of my actions on deployment, and I served with honor. But that does not diminish the ache of caring for others and not being able to help them.

I've done plenty of bad things in life, I've had lots of stories I could put in this space, but I think it's important to see some of the unique ways that moral injury shows up through the lens of a leader. It's not always an acute injury; sometimes it's a slow fracture—the sound of your wheel crackling under the weight of something your hands can't fix.

This matters because it doesn't just happen in war. That same fracture can follow you to the sideline, the classroom, the hospital, or the patrol car. Sometimes it's what you *couldn't do to help*—the choices you had to make, the boundaries you held, the resources you lacked, the rules you couldn't change, the person you couldn't pull up.

Moral injury is the psychological, emotional, and spiritual distress that arises when a person's actions—or their inability to act—collide with their deeply held moral code, values, or sense of rightness.[15] It isn't only reconciling your own wrongdoing; it's also the anguish of witnessing harm, feeling betrayed by what should be right, or being powerless to prevent suffering.

There are so many ways we can experience moral injury, many self-inflicted, others not. Regardless, when moral injury is present, the spaghetti junction of leadership and trauma can grow more tangled. We're taught to stay composed, to lead with strength, to carry the mission forward. But no one tells you what to do when the mission and your heart collide and moral injury leaves cracks in us. That's a hidden cost of leading in the dark.

But cracks don't mean collapse—they mean the system's under pressure and calling for repair. Moral repair, to me, isn't a theory; it's the daily work of restoring integrity after it's been shaken. It starts with truth, realignment to what I value most, and doing good again—serving, teaching, leading, loving, and forgiving myself for being human in moments that asked for more than I had to give.

EXCUSES AND THE QUIET SLIDE

When that deployment ended in 2004, I returned to come home to play basketball at the University of Texas at Dallas. I remember my teammates and I taking a trip to Austin to hang out. On the surface, life had moved on. Inside, I was still replaying the moments I couldn't repair, and the people I couldn't save.

On that trip, we were outside of a bar on Austin's famous Sixth Street when I heard an accent that I knew immediately. I asked if he was Iraqi, and he lit up and said yes. I matched his energy and was excited to ask what part of Iraq he was from. I was feeling good that night, and I didn't expect to freeze when he said, "Basra."

Basra was the city I'd watched light up during *Shock and Awe*—the first night of the war. He told me how grateful he was to be in America, how he finally felt safe here. I wanted to share that joy with him. But I couldn't. Because I knew what he had lived through, and I watched the bombs drop and knew he was on the other side of that same night. I know he was thankful and happy to be here, but I couldn't help but think that it didn't erase what had happened to his home.

He thanked me for serving and said he wouldn't be here without soldiers like me, and for some reason, I crumbled. For him, it was a moment of fellowship, of appreciation, and a moment where he was happy. But I couldn't hear it. In this happy, healthy Iraqi man, having fun at a bar in America, I could only see the people I left behind. The destruction of war surrounding so many good humans. The good people I couldn't bring with me. The kind people I couldn't help.

I willingly went on three deployments to a combat zone, and I would do it again if I were needed. I am not antiwar. But my desire to go to war is driven by love, not hate. Love for good people who need to be protected from bad things. I believe this is critical to understand, because I have felt this in other spaces. When we serve, in any capacity, and that service is driven by love, seeing good people whom we can't help can wound us deeply.

I didn't have a language or understanding of it as a college kid at a bar, but that was moral injury finding its voice. The wound hurt, so I drowned it out as fast as I could with as much beer as possible that night. In case you were wondering, *this is not a helpful action.*

No matter how much beer I drank, trying to hide it, what remained was the ache of knowing I'd tried to do good, but harm had still happened in my shadow. The war had ended, but the cracks had followed me home, and I didn't even know how to name what was breaking. And what you don't see as broken, you can't repair.

As I went down that road, I just thought I was sad and that no one at home could understand me. So I did not share. My choice to be quiet became isolation, and isolation became avoidance. Eventually, I started sitting alone on my back patio at night with a six-pack beside me, replaying everything I couldn't fix.

I wasn't chasing peace. I was chasing punishment.

I told myself the choices I was making were acceptable because of where I had come home from. My friends and family did not know what I was dealing with, so they did not challenge me either. And that's how excuses start—soft, reasonable, almost kind. People hand them to you freely, especially when you've seen a lot.[16]

"You've been through enough."

"You deserve a break."

"No one expects you to be perfect."

"I can't imagine what that was like."

But excuses lower your standards to what you are actually capable of, and once you pick them up, they are hard to put down. They whisper, *Stay numb. Stay still. Stay small.* They somehow let your ego be fully satisfied with absolute mediocrity. *Look how well you are able to survive. You've endured so much. Just getting through is special.*

For a while, I listened. My life was still moving, but I wasn't. That's when I realized something: I wasn't avoiding pain, I was killing purpose, and I was playing small. I was merely enduring suffering and excusing the fact that, rather than giving my best to the world, I was simply existing. Thankfully, God whispered His plans, reminding me that a life of impact, expression, growth, and service to others was the only way I wanted to live.

But if excuses had their way, I'd be OK with my *Absolute. Very. Least. Effort.*

THE DISCIPLINED FOUR S'S: TAKE COMMAND OF YOUR LIFE

Avoidant, isolated, six-pack-on-the-corner-of-a-back-patio nights were never going to repair the growing cracks I had. There had to be intentional movement in a better direction. I needed to seek wholeness through healthy choices to fight my way back to being the me I wanted to be in this world. But the fight for wholeness can't just live in your head. You can't think your way out of the dark—you have to move your way through it. For me, that movement began with four small, steady anchors. They weren't fancy, and they didn't belong in a textbook. They were simply the things that helped me rebuild my wheel, one spoke at a time.

Sweat. Spirit. Substance. Sleep.

I first heard the idea as a young sergeant as I listened to a command sergeant major talk about "the three S's: sweat, spirit, and substance." She said, "Get those right in your life, and you'll be successful."

I knew that was simple brilliance, but I was twenty-five, and I didn't practice the discipline to live it yet. Years later, when the cracks started showing beyond what I could hide, and I had to fight my way back to steady ground, I finally took her words to heart.

If I wanted success, I had to make some changes in my life, and I knew exactly where to start.

SWEAT

Movement is medicine. It doesn't have to be extreme as long as it is consistent. Some of my best prayers have been whispered between sets or during a long run when my thoughts finally outran my excuses. When you move your body, you remind your mind that you're still alive and you are capable of thriving. There's a ton of science you don't need me to repeat that we all know is true: Working out raises endorphins. If you want to be happy, start with a sweat.

SPIRIT

This isn't necessarily about religion; it's about alignment inside. It's the quiet check-in with the part of yourself that still believes in something bigger than yourself. For me, it's prayer, gratitude, reflection, and con-nection to God. Sometimes it's just intentional silence and calming my thoughts to align with my purpose and get in tune with the direction of my life. Spirit speaks loudest in silence, growth, and reflection. But my spirit also loves to be compounded by sweat.

SUBSTANCE

Everything you allow in—mentally, physically, emotionally, and relationally—either strengthens or sabotages you. Whether it's food, drink, media, conversations, or relationships, be intentional about what you *feed yourself.* What you consume becomes what you carry. Some things are fine in moderation. Some are worth building into every day. And some are simply poison.

Fill your mind, body, and circle with what builds you. Stay away from what harms you.

When life hits hard, whatever's in you is what comes out. Pressure doesn't lie—it exposes what you've been feeding yourself, so guard what you take in, and stay intentional with consuming what builds you, not what just quiets your storm.

SLEEP

I had to add this fourth *S* to the sergeant major's version, because we all need this one. No one talks enough about what exhaustion does to leaders. You can't fight your battles—or your demons—on fumes. Sleep isn't a weakness. It's recovery. Rest is where repair begins. It's the binding that allows your other spokes to hold.

DISCIPLINE

When you are disciplined and steady in those habits, you are simply a stronger version of the person you want to be. The stronger we are, the better our integrity holds, and the more we eliminate excuses and call ourselves on our own messes. Discipline is part of wholeness because it makes space for repair in motion through one healthy decision at a time.

It's a lifelong journey, and the four S's are *simple*, but they're not *easy* unless we practice them consistently. This is the kind of discipline that starts before motivation shows up. We do it because we know we need to, not always because we want to. But we know that discipline isn't punishment. It is *order*. It's the quiet act of bringing your life back under *your own command*. You can't lead others if you've surrendered command of your own house.

THE FOUR S'S ARROW CHECK

There's no finish line—only forward.
- *Note Your Position:* Rate where you are *today* in each S.
- *Mark Your Inches:* Identify one small move—an inch—that nudges each arrow forward.
  - ▷ Sweat → Move your body, even for five minutes.
  - ▷ Spirit → Pause for gratitude, prayer, or silence.
  - ▷ Substance → Feed your body and mind with things that strengthen, not poison.
  - ▷ Sleep → Protect recovery like you protect readiness.
- *Repeat:* Momentum doesn't start fast. It's gained in inches, which are bought through consistent, disciplined action. Small wins stack. Direction matters more than distance.

The Four S's Arrow Check

THE WHOLENESS BLUEPRINT

When you are at the intersection of leadership and trauma, the road gets messy. I used moral injury as one concept to highlight how it's easy to end up going the wrong direction. But it really is a spaghetti junction. There are so many turns you can take, so many variables in each story. Some paths serve you. Some steal your fight.

If I can offer one simple blueprint to check when you can't slow down and you are in the middle of mess, it is to consider your wholeness blueprint to make sure you are capable of continuing on your journey without breaking down.

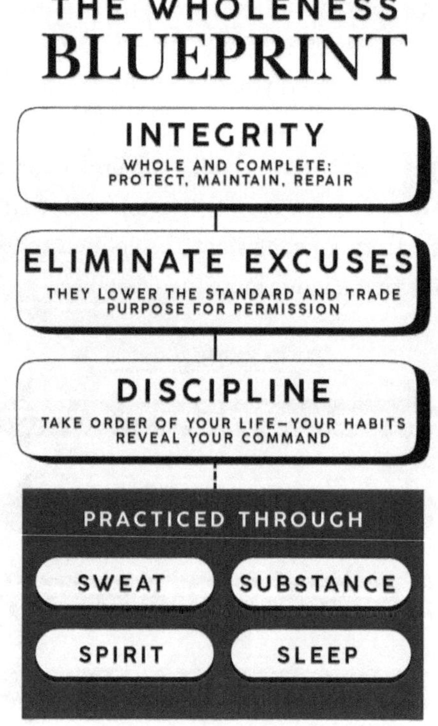

The Wholeness Blueprint

Integrity is what keeps you whole and complete. Eliminating excuses—without shame—raises the standard for what you're capable of. Discipline protects that strength. And the four S's are how you practice those core personal disciplines.

Sweat. Spirit. Substance. Sleep.

They aren't just habits. They're how you take command of your own life. Because when your daily order collapses, your integrity eventually follows. Discipline isn't about perfection. It's about maintaining structure under pressure. And structure is what allows you to lead with strength when everything else feels uncertain.

Disciplined leaders are built to travel stronger.

Whole leaders are built to travel longer.

LEADERSHIP LENS

Wholeness Under Load

Leadership under trauma doesn't break you all at once. It can fracture you quietly—in moments where you care deeply and can't make things right.

That kind of injury doesn't mean you've failed. It means you've been carrying weight that mattered.

Wholeness isn't purity. It's structure that holds under uneven pressure.

Leaders stay whole not by avoiding cracks, but by noticing them early, tending them honestly, and refusing to let injury turn into drift.

This is the work beneath the work—staying aligned enough to keep moving when the road offers no clear direction or stopping point.

TACTICAL TAKEAWAY

Navigate the Junction

- *Name the Injury.* When something in you tightens, numbs, or goes quiet, don't rush past it. What you can name, you can tend. What you ignore, you can't repair.
- *Repair in Motion.* You don't need a full stop to realign. One honest action in the right direction restores more strength than waiting for clarity.
- *Reclaim Discipline.* The 4 S's—*Sweat, Spirit, Substance, Sleep*—aren't fixes—they're maintenance. They keep you capable of staying present when leadership demands don't slow down.
- *Eliminate Excuses.* Excuses trade purpose for permission. Don't lower the standard—repair what's slipping and keep moving.
- *Endure Forward.* Progress, not perfection, keeps the wheel turning. Check your spokes, stay the course toward your mission, and roll.

PART III

THE FIGHT

*Light doesn't signal victory—
it reveals the mission.
Lead with scars that still shine,
and move with purpose.*

CHAPTER 9

MENTAL TOUGHNESS AND RELENTLESS OPTIMISM

I WAS SITTING IN my cinder block office, tucked beneath the stadium seating of our basketball arena, when I got the call. A week earlier, during my biopsy, my doctor said, "If it's nothing, we'll text. If it's something, I'll call." I had prayed for a text. But there I was on the phone as she said, "I encourage you to be *cautiously* optimistic."

It was cancer.

Her voice was calm and clinical, with words landing like Charlie Brown's teacher, muffled and far away. I barely heard anything until that phrase.

When we hung up, I sat in the quiet. My biggest fear wasn't surgery or treatment, it was telling my wife, Jess. She'd been urging me for years to get that spot checked, and I felt like I'd failed her—failed us—by waiting until it threatened everything we'd built together. But I couldn't sit in that fear long because it was time to decide how I wanted to fight, and who I wanted to be in the middle of it. So, I scoffed at the term cautiously optimistic and thought: *Optimistic, absolutely. Cautious? No, thank you*. I wasn't going to live under a banner of caution. I would be *relentlessly optimistic*. Period.

THE SEED I FORGOT ABOUT

A year earlier, I had picked up a book that quickly became a favorite: *The Art of Becoming Oneself* by Dr. Jim Brennan.[17]

Just from reading his back cover, he felt like a kindred spirit and a mentor I didn't yet know I needed. Brennan is a human performance and emotional intelligence expert, and during one of the winningest decades in NCAA history, he was the sports psychologist for the Villanova men's basketball program. He's also a fellow United States Army military police officer. He turned twenty in Vietnam; I turned twenty-one in Iraq. Different wars, similar weight carried home. A unique understanding of grief, anger, and moral injury. And, of course, we both love basketball.

I devoured his book on vacation the year prior and was drawn in to chapter 13: "Relentless Optimism." I absorbed it, loved it, and then set it aside, carrying it quietly in the background of my life without even realizing it.

Fast-forward to after my diagnosis, I was in the middle of the very first row machine workout after my surgeries healed, when I caught sight of the cover of Dr. Brennan's book on the shelf. Something in me knew I needed to open it. I paused, set the handle down, walked over, and picked it up. Mid-workout, catching my breath, I flipped through, and there it was: chapter 13. I froze, and my eyes got big, and I literally laughed at myself. For weeks, I'd been telling people *relentless optimism* was my cancer-fighting slogan. I was convinced I'd coined it in the heat of the fight and in sheer defiance of the word *caution*. In reality, Brennan had planted that seed in me a year earlier, right in the middle of one of my new favorite books. I just hadn't noticed it had taken root.

The next week, from my treatment chair—Harry Porter, the port in my left shoulder, hooked up and doing its job—I pulled out my phone, did some research, and sent Dr. Brennan an email. I told him the story, how I thought I had come up with the phrase, and how it turned out that he'd given it to me long before I needed it. He wrote back almost immediately. He told me that's exactly what he hoped his work would do—plant seeds that might bloom in someone's life when the storms came.

That's exactly what he'd done. Relentless optimism is a powerful toughness tool in life. I always believed in it, but I needed to have some dirt and storms in life to see what grew out of that belief. What has grown is a better version of myself. One that is tougher, more determined, more passionate, and more inspired to do more with my time. But it started with a determination that I would be both highly aggressive and stubbornly positive with what life brought my way in the road ahead, and it continued into a belief that life is about more than merely enduring and getting through pain and struggle. It is about being the absolute best version of myself and expressing myself with fullness of life through it. Relentless optimism is not a peppy presence of positivity. It is a gritty toughness born of a self-determination to make the most out of every moment, no matter what you face. It is the ultimate form of toughness, and it is where mental toughness begins.

EXPERT VOICE—DR. JIM BRENNAN ON RELENTLESS OPTIMISM

"Relentless optimism is a response to adversity that can be both highly aggressive and stubbornly positive. It's not wishful thinking—it's seeing the truth of the situation and deciding you will create the best possible outcome anyway. It's a whole-hearted acceptance in the face of difficulty, using life's hardships to wake yourself up, not put yourself to sleep. The purpose of life is to go forward."

—DR. JIM BRENNAN, *The Art of Becoming Oneself*

THE HILL

At the start of my cancer-fighting journey, when my oncologist laid out the next steps—scans, surgery, lymph node testing, and a year of infusions every three weeks—I found inspiration from another leader who had modeled toughness for me in life: SFC Edward Dale Davis.

Before I served with him in Iraq, Davis had been a United States Marine in Vietnam. On July 6, 1967, his company came under attack by a numerically superior North Vietnamese force. His platoon was pinned down in a valley by heavy machine-gun fire coming from a hill.

Davis didn't wait for orders. With complete disregard for his own safety, he advanced across open, fire-swept terrain—rifle in hand, grenades flying—charging the enemy position. He killed four North Vietnamese soldiers, destroyed the machine-gun nest, and then held his ground under intense fire to prevent the enemy from overrunning his unit. His actions saved countless Marines and allowed medics to reach the wounded.

For that day, he was awarded the Silver Star, one of the nation's most distinguished awards for valor in combat. And somehow, I got to go to war with that man and witness how he approached a fight.

The official narrative described his actions as demonstrating "a calm presence of mind and aggressiveness."[18] That line described him perfectly because he was always steady under fire and decisive when it mattered.

In Iraq, we learned to read him. If Davis was calm, we were OK. If he got tight, we knew it was time to move. But we learned early, when the fight is on, you don't hesitate: *You take the hill.*

So I made myself a promise: Every time I went for treatment, I would run the stairs instead of taking the elevator. Blood draw on floor two. Infusion on floor three. Those stairs became my hill.

I didn't run them because I felt strong. I ran them because I knew this was my fight and I was going to charge into it with a calm mind and an aggressive posture.

Davis's lessons didn't reflect traditional mental toughness models, but he gave me one of the lessons I needed most. What he lived out was the kind of mental toughness that only emerges in unimaginable fights when the odds are stacked against you—a rare balance of calm presence of mind and fierce action when it mattered most.

PRESENCE PROFILE— CALM + AGGRESSIVE

In chaos, leaders can't be too calm or too aggressive. When you lean to the extreme side of calm, people think you're disengaged. If you come in too hot and overly aggressive, you create more chaos.

**Calm + Aggressive =
Trustworthy Under Pressure.**

It's the leader who can look at the battlefield—or the scoreboard, or the scan results—with clear eyes, then still point to the dangerous hill that must be climbed and say, "Charge!"

THE MILITARY'S MENTAL TOUGHNESS MODEL

The stairs toward treatment were my hill. But they weren't the only place where my relentless optimism was being tested.

That same year, between cancer treatments, I was deep into my doctoral work at Creighton University. I almost put my school on pause when I got my diagnosis, but it ended up being a very positive space for me to keep an eye on my future, even through the brain fog. In course after course, the same name kept appearing in my reading: Dr. Martin Seligman.

At first, I barely noticed. Then I couldn't ignore it.

I kept running into his work from different angles. In leadership research. In psychology. And then again in *Grit* by Angela Duckworth, where I learned that Seligman—her mentor—had challenged her to move beyond toughness alone and study perseverance through struggle. Grit, I realized, wasn't just force.[19] It was sustained effort fueled by belief.

Eventually, I picked up Seligman's book *The Hope Circuit*.[20] There, he laid out something that stopped me cold: The will to take action in the face of suffering hinges on one thing—hope—the belief that your actions can create a better future. Hope, he argued, doesn't soften effort. It drives it. Without it, people slide into helplessness.

I had never heard it put that way before—but he had the science to back what already made sense.

As I kept reading, the connection didn't feel accidental. It felt like something I was finally being given language for—something I'd already lived before I could name it. Seligman wasn't just a researcher. He was the architect of the US Army's Master Resilience Training (MRT) program—the same program I had trained in during the latter half of my twenty years in uniform. Preparing soldiers to be mentally tough before they ever step into the fight. Giving us tools to move toward growth after trauma—otherwise known as post-traumatic growth (PTG[21])—and to mitigate the threat of post-traumatic stress disorder (PTSD) in response to combat trauma.[22]

That hadn't always been the case.

I flashed back to 2003 in a waiting room filled with my battle buddies at Fort Hood, demobilizing after Iraq. We were handed questionnaires meant to identify who might need mental health support. On paper, they were there to help. In reality, the message moved quietly through the ranks, whispered from chair to chair: *Don't fill them out honestly. You don't want to get flagged. You don't want to get stuck here. You didn't see anything. You didn't do anything. You're fine.*

It was the unspoken leadership lesson of the times—how to avoid being coded as broken and keep moving.

But the war on terror taught us hard lessons. PTSD and suicide rates were climbing to devastating levels. The Army needed more than crisis intervention—it needed proactive, preventive tools to build resilience and mental toughness before and after combat.

Dr. Seligman answered that call. Master Resilience Training taught soldiers to identify unhelpful thought patterns, shift perspectives, and deliberately train optimism—not as fluff, but as a combat readiness skill.

Years later, during my cancer journey, I picked up a *Harvard Business Review* piece on mental toughness.[23] The opening line was bolded and unmistakable:

Optimism is the key.

There he was again, but this time, with my new favorite word.

Across war, leadership research, and personal survival, the message was consistent. Real toughness wasn't about hardening yourself or pretending pain didn't exist. It was about maintaining the belief that you still had agency—that forward movement was possible, even when the road was brutal.

That truth connected every thread for me—the science of Seligman, the wisdom of Brennan, and the personal fight I was embracing. From different worlds, the message was the same: Real strength doesn't come from hardening; it comes from hope. It's not about denying fear or pretending pain doesn't exist, but about believing you still have the power to move forward through it and finding the good anyway.

That's the version of toughness I know. Not barked orders or clenched fists. There is a time for that kind of fight, but that's not at the heart of mental toughness. It is not silence or suppression. But a steadiness that holds you upright when the world shakes.

For too long, we've confused toughness with tension and grit with grimness. The toughest people I've ever known weren't the ones who scowled through the storm. They were the ones who steadied their breathing, lifted their eyes, and said, "Let's go."

Mental toughness isn't cold. It's charged with hope. It isn't the absence of fear; it's the belief that what's in front of you can still be faced.

That's why optimism isn't a soft skill. It's a combat skill. And the leaders who train it will outlast the ones who don't.

LEADERSHIP LENS

The Optimism Edge

Mental toughness isn't about clenching your jaw and pretending you're fine. It's about *disciplining your perspective*—choosing what story you'll believe when the world starts to shake.

Optimism isn't a mood. It's a method. It's the trained ability to find one fact that proves forward motion is possible and to build from there. When leaders live that way—acknowledging the storm but steering toward the light—they give everyone around them permission to hope again.

It's not naive. It's necessary. It's not a motto or a T-shirt slogan. It's **combat-tested** and now **cancer-tested** leadership—the kind forged in foxholes, hospital rooms, and locker rooms— any place where people are watching to see if you still believe.

Too many leaders burn out because they confuse toughness with tension. They hold everything in until something breaks. But real toughness breathes, adapts, and leads with relentless optimism.

Name your hill. Charge it. Keep moving until it's yours.

TACTICAL TAKEAWAY

Relentless in Motion

- *See the ground.* Don't sugarcoat the situation—call it what it is. Truth is the starting line of every fight worth winning.

- *Adjust your aim.* Once you see the problem, turn your focus to what can be done, not what can't. You empower what you look at and give yourself agency in your own life.
- *Respond. Don't react.* Feel your emotions to events and actions, but don't let them drive your bus (Nod to rule number one of *The Energy Bus* by Jon Gordon).[24] Anger, fear, and resentment are loud but can take you off the road. Only you control your response.
- *Express. Don't endure.* Enduring protects you; expressing propels you. Move toward your passions, your purpose, your mission, and your best self.
- *Advance from here.* Wherever *here* is, decide this is the point where you will move forward from.

Relentless optimism isn't blind faith—it's a decision. It's the practice of believing there's still something you can build, even when the world says you're done.

SCARS, SYMPTOMS, AND STRENGTH

SOME SCARS NEVER go away.

I have a big scar on my calf from fighting cancer. Most days I barely notice it, but some days, I bump it and realize it's still tender—maybe always will be. Some people see it and notice I must have gone through something, but that scar reminds me that I survived something that could have killed me. It slowed me down, but it also made me stronger, more grateful, and more urgent about leading intentionally while I still have time.

Grief and trauma can feel the same. They often leave marks that are tender, sometimes invisible, sometimes life-saving reminders. You don't erase them. When you have a painful scar, you learn to live with it, handle it with care if necessary, and move in another way that may not hurt as badly when it's hit. When you learn to navigate the scar, you can learn to appreciate life on the other side of it.

But it is still there. Sometimes it stings, sometimes you barely notice, and sometimes it reshapes your whole life. If you let it, it can reshape it for the better, despite the wound that may hurt and feels like it may never fully heal anytime it gets *hit*.

When I look at my scar from cancer, I think of my journey with PTSD.

For years, I tried to make sense of where I fit on the bell curve of trauma. Dr. Martin Seligman describes how trauma responses tend to fall into three sides of the bell curve: PTSD on the left, resilience in the middle, and growth on the right.[25]

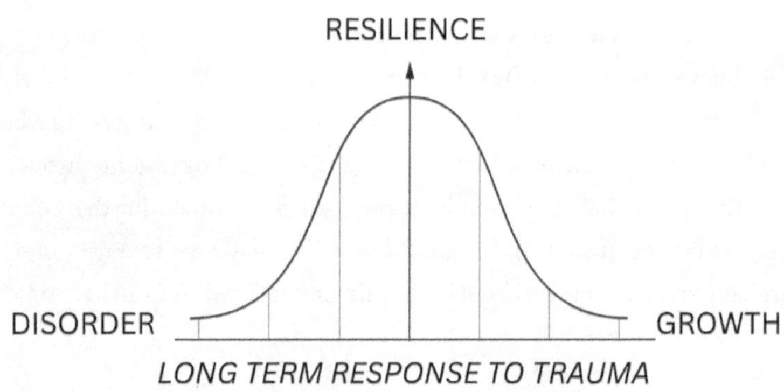

When I first heard it from a man I so deeply respect, that picture helped me. It gave me words to explain what felt impossible, and it gave me peace knowing that most people find resilience after trauma. I know understanding this helps some people in the same way it helped me understand that their post-traumatic stress symptoms are normal. That most people find resilience after trauma at some point and that they are no different. There can be such a weight lifted in understanding that those heavy and hard challenges are normal, and most people find resilience. And, I fully believe this concept to be true.

I also believe some will suffer from severe PTSD, and some will experience growth, and our choices, actions, behaviors, beliefs, and habits greatly shape that. In other words, our response to the trauma, not the trauma itself, will dramatically impact how we experience and live through the trauma, no matter what it is.

But, after being around so many great leaders who have had complex, hard, layered trauma, there's still something missing from that conversation for me, and I can finally name it.

THE PATIO AND THE DIAGNOSIS

At my worst, I was living squarely on the left of the bell curve. In 2010, I'd sit in the dark corner of my backyard patio with a beer in my hand, swallowed up by thoughts that I'd never find my place in the world again. I had been to war. I had seen violence up close. I had come home and jumped straight into coaching—the dream job I thought would keep me afloat and return me to normalcy. But when the noise of basketball season faded, the chaos of my mind grew louder.

I navigated heavy, hard PTSD alone, silently, for far longer than I may ever realize.[26] If you scrolled through a Mayo Clinic website, I was a walking model of the symptoms list.

Years later, I found myself in a doctor's office sharing my struggle for the first time after checking a box on a Veterans Affairs form. I was finally willing to formally ask the question I had avoided for most of my life. After feeling fully exposed to a psychologist I had never met and going down a laundry list of questions and stories, I fearfully asked, "Do I have PTSD?"

"Yes," he said. "But you're very resilient."

Tears streamed down my face as I said thank you, trying to swallow the wave of emotion long enough to figure out if I was sad or proud.

Hearing the words "Yes, but you are resilient" hit something deep. When I got in the car, I broke down completely. I still don't have a word for what those tears carried—it felt like my entire soul had been seen. I'd held that fear in silence for years, and now it was out in the open—but with something new beside it. PTSD and resilience. Both true. Both me.

That moment reframed everything. I wasn't either/or. I was both/and.

And if you've ever sat in the dark and wondered, *What if I'm broken? How will I lead?* I know that feeling. But sometimes the most freeing truth is that you can carry scars and have triggers and still stand tall. You can hold a diagnosis in one hand and return to and find resilience in the other. You can be both/and, too. And the choices we make after that fact often determine the trajectory of where we settle into the bell curve for the long haul.

The stronger I get, the more I move to the right side of that curve. The less the word PTSD grips me, the more I see that what Dr. Seligman sketched out wasn't just theory—it was a map. Leaders who navigate trauma live somewhere along that bell curve between stress and growth, shifting right and left depending on the season of grief or stress response we're in, combined with the choices we are making.

Tedeschi and Calhoun originally gave that far-right space a name— *post-traumatic growth*—and I shy away from sharing that potential with people in the middle of pain and grief, but I know it exists.[27] I've seen it in my soldiers, in my players, and in the mirror. There can be growth in the aftermath of trauma.

You don't outrun trauma. The scar does not go away. You evolve within it. You learn to let the scar remind you not of what broke you, but of what you did with it in spite of the pain.

MY WIFE'S WAKE-UP CALL

Fast-forward to 2025. My wife—Captain Brittain, a nineteen-year veteran police officer—came home from a peer-support training where a police widow told the story of losing her husband to suicide after years of invisible trauma.

My wife has always been steady: salt-of-the-earth, West Texas farm-girl grit—the kind of woman who doesn't flinch at much. But that night, she looked at me and admitted, "We see murders, suicides, violence, trauma day after day. We never get to unsee it. If we struggle, we worry if we're still fit to do the job. And if we can't do the job, we lose our sense of purpose. Of course, we could have PTSD. I just didn't realize so many of these symptoms were so common to me and those I love. I need to pay more attention—to myself and to those I lead. Any one of us could be him."

Her words stopped me. Because within them, I *felt* the same unspoken fear that once drove me to that patio: *What if I'm broken? How could I not be?*

What I wanted her to hear—and what I wish I had heard sooner—is this: Symptoms don't cancel strength. You can struggle and still serve. You can feel it all and still lead with resilience.

SIGNALS AND SOLUTIONS

When I came home from Iraq in 2004, I threw up almost every morning for a year. I didn't know it then, but it was my nervous system staging for a battle that wasn't there—blood rushing to my arms and legs, gearing up to fight. PTSD and the prolonged fight-or-flight response are real.[28]

My body told me what my mind couldn't admit. Sometimes your body knows you need help before you do.

Eventually, I learned simple tools like *box breathing* to reset my system: Inhale for four, hold for four, exhale for four, hold for four.[29]

Years later, I saw one of my athletes slipping away quietly to the trash can before games when she knew a college scout was there to see her. Everyone thought she was sick, but I recognized the signs of a heightened stress response that looked a lot like mine. I pulled her aside: "Look at me. Box breathe. In four. Hold four. Out four. Hold four."

She didn't need the science. She didn't need my war stories. She just needed breath and the right tools to get her stress response in check. I don't think we ever even talked about it, but I appreciated that she trusted me and followed my breath. She crushed that game, and she's still playing in college today.

Wouldn't it be great if we were all that coachable? If we were more receptive to the things that actually serve us—tools that help our bodies and minds respond better in the middle of heightened stress. I know I would have saved myself from a lot of suffering and more than a few bad decisions.

FUEL FOR THE FIGHT

Beyond trauma response and creating the Army-wide resilience training program, Dr. Seligman studied a phenomenon he called the "Hope Circuit."[30] His conclusion was simple but powerful: People resist helplessness when they believe their efforts to end suffering can make a difference.

That's where hope is born—not from wishful thinking, but from the belief that our actions matter. If you believe that nothing you do can end the struggles you face, it is much more likely that you will give up. But if you're shown tools, strategies, or supports that can lighten the weight, even a little, hope begins to flicker. And once hope is present, it fuels will. Will makes us act. And action pulls us toward resilience instead of helplessness.

The hope that drives my resilience has rarely come in story-worthy moments. It usually arrived as small glimmers—a shared belly laugh from an old friend, snuggling with my dog Sarge, smiling at a random kid making faces at me from a car at a stoplight. Those flickers reminded me: There is still life to smile at, there is still light. Even in the dark. And, since that is true, maybe there is more I should be enjoying.

Those little moments of hope give space for the numbness and helplessness to weaken long enough to build your will. Inch by inch, you gain momentum and strength where this whole thing started in the prologue—the *Warrior Triangle*. In short:

- *Self*—the determination and discipline to train, study, move, grow, and keep my life in order—anchored in purpose and will, not chaos.
- *A Squad of Foxhole Friends*—the people I can count on to be by my side when the night is darkest and the assault is the hardest.
- *Tapping into the Spirit of Having Faith and Following the Whispers*— the quiet reminders from God, from prayer, from deep places in my spirit that remind me I'm not alone and that there is a plan for my life, even if I don't see it yet.

When one side weakens, the other sides hold me up. Sometimes only one side remained strong while the others faltered, but that one would carry me through until all three could flourish again. When all three sides are strong, hope has room to thrive, will stays alive, and resilience builds momentum. They say hope is a muscle that needs training—I agree. We build that strength by embracing the full power of the Warrior Triangle.

PTSD SYMPTOMS TO WATCH FOR

Common post-traumatic stress symptoms may include the following:[31]

- Nightmares or intrusive memories that don't fade
- Feeling constantly on edge or jumpy
- Avoiding people, places, or reminders of the event
- Emotional numbness, guilt, or shame that lingers
- Trouble sleeping or concentrating
- Anger, reckless behavior, or shutting down

These symptoms don't mean you're weak—they mean you're human. Most fade over time with healthy coping, but if they don't, it's a sign to bring in backup.

WHEN IT'S TIME FOR BACKUP

Tools matter, but there are moments when tools aren't enough. Bring in backup when you experience the following:[32]

- The weight never lifts, and the symptoms keep stacking for more than one month.
- Sleep, relationships, or work start to unravel.
- Alcohol, drugs, or risky behaviors become the outlet and coping choice.
- Thoughts of self-harm or suicide creep in.

*If you or someone you know is in crisis, call or text **988** to reach the Suicide and Crisis Lifeline in the United States.*

Remember: Needing help doesn't mean you're out of the fight—it means you're fighting smarter. No athlete plays through serious injury without treatment or telling a coach they are hurt. Trauma is no different.

CLOSING TRUTHS

Here's what I know now:

- Scars may hurt, but they don't have to scare you.
- You can navigate PTSD or carry significant post-traumatic symptoms and still be resilient.
- You can hold grief and still be gritty toward a better life.

- Trauma impacts you, but it doesn't decide your fate.
- Comparing your trauma or how you carry your trauma doesn't serve you. But learning from the successes and failures of others (without judgment or guilt) can serve you.

Last and maybe most important: It may not feel kind to say it out loud to someone who is struggling, but I'd rather be real than kind here. Our choices matter, and we are responsible for them, no matter what we face. Excuses are poison to progress. Excuses are kind killers of will and self-respect. Don't let them in.

How you respond to what happens in your life often determines whether you remain stuck in disorder or find steadiness in resilience.

Like the scar on my leg, trauma may never fully disappear. But it can become a reminder that you're still here, still moving, still able to live strong, resilient, and even joyful—*stacking hope* and building the will to win *one choice at a time.*

LEADERSHIP LENS

We spend so much time trying to hide what hurt us that we forget scars are evidence of survival. They mean you've healed enough to keep moving. Being strong doesn't mean you haven't been touched by trauma; it just means you've been rebuilt from it. The deeper truth is that the parts of us we once called damaged often become the most dependable parts of our design.

Symptoms remind us we're still human: the sleepless nights, the overthinking, the ache that shows up without warning. They're not proof of failure—they're proof of impact. Leadership leaves marks. But when you stop seeing those marks as disqualifications and start seeing them as credentials, you stop leading from perfection and start leading from presence.

TACTICAL TAKEAWAY

1. When an old wound flares up, don't hide it. Acknowledge it as information, not identity.
2. Use your scars as teaching tools—stories that show others what endurance looks like.
3. Rest when symptoms surface; repair is part of readiness.
4. Remind yourself: Scars are signs of the battle, not weakness.

The strongest leaders aren't the ones who've avoided pain—they're the ones who've pushed it into purpose.

CHAPTER 11

MOVE FORWARD

I WENT TO WATCH the movie *Black Hawk Down* when I was eighteen years old. As I sat there watching a story of heroism, grit, and leadership in dark times, my young mind kept staring at the backward flag on the soldiers' sleeves. I remember thinking, *This movie is incredible, but who messed up the uniforms? The costume department should be fired—all the flags are backward!*

I didn't know what I didn't know. What I learned later—once I wore the uniform myself—is that there's a reason the flag appears to fly backward on a soldier's right shoulder. To anyone unfamiliar, it looks like a mistake, like the stars are on the wrong side. But to soldiers, it means something unshakable: The flag faces that way because it's always charging *forward.*

Imagine carrying a flag while charging into battle toward the fight— that's the direction it flies. No matter the obstacle, no matter the struggle, our flag is always advancing. Never retreating. It is the essence of the *fighting spirit.* The disciplined trajectory of how you're expected to face conflict. *Forward. Toward the fight. Always advancing. Never retreat.*

THE GRITTY ONES

Many of my favorite humans—the most gritty, resilient, determined, and inspiring souls I know—have faced unimaginable hardships. They're the ones the world tried to break, yet they still carry a light in their eyes and joy in their hearts. These people are magnetic, as if they possess secret wisdom we all want to unlock. I've learned volumes just by watching how they walk, talk, and shoulder their burdens.

I'm thankful for those people and their lessons because I needed them as I faced the hard, heavier parts of life: Combat tours in Iraq, ramp ceremonies with soldiers coming home under a flag, losing students, losing friends, fighting cancer, and fighting myself. I've lived in the swing of the oscillating fan—from grit to grief, from fight to fatigue. I've picked up the heavy because it was mine to carry. I set it down when I had to rest. And I've taken the long road that taught me the discipline of doing both—without shame. I now know that resilience isn't always about sprinting through the fire. Sometimes it's giving space for sadness. Recognizing moral injury. Reflecting. Reframing. Cultivating gratitude. Choosing hope and optimism anyway—and fighting to choose joy when it would be easier to just feel the pain.

It's about choosing where the next step goes, even when you can't see the rest of the road. And the best way to find your next step when you feel like the last one was clearly wrong is to learn how to be a Next Best Action (NBA) Player.

THE NEXT BEST ACTION PLAYERS

I heard a brilliant teaching concept used at a Point Guard College (PGC) session that I immediately stuck into my toolbox for my own team.[33] When my players have a bad play, a bad game, make a mistake—or just take a beating while facing adversity—we have a mantra: We are *NBA Players*. Next. Best. Action. Players.

In leadership, in life, and in loss, the win isn't in doing everything perfectly. It's not even in doing everything fast. The way to win is the sum of continuously taking the next best action again and again—after failure, after mistake, after loss. We play in the NBA. If we are grounded, present, and aligned with our values and integrity—and free from excuses—the direction of that *next best action* is often clearer. It may still be foggy and uncertain, but you only need one step forward to continue the journey.

Sometimes it is aggressively charging the hill to face the fight ahead of you. Sometimes it's quiet prayer and reflection. Sometimes it's showing up to practice the day after hosting a funeral. Sometimes it's having the conversation no one else wants to have. Sometimes it's moving an inch in your choices with your 4S's. And sometimes the most courageous move of all, if you find yourself struggling, is to ask for help.

Forward isn't always loud. Forward isn't always visible. Forward is direction—actions aligned with intention. Forward is a mustard seed of faith that, even in your most *numb and hollow spaces*, maybe, just maybe, *miracles are made in inches.*

And by the way—if you don't know which step forward is right, but you're doing your best to find it, here's the truth: Trying *is* right. Stop doubting. Stop judging. Keep reflecting, praying, hoping, trying—and even if you take an intentional tactical pause, that's OK. But when that pause is done, Just. Keep. Moving. Forward.

REFLECTION CHECK

- What's your next *move* that keeps your compass true?
- What would *forward* look like for you today?

LEADERSHIP LENS

Forward isn't a destination; it's a discipline. It's the decision to keep moving with what you've learned, even when the weight still lingers. There's no perfect closure—only continued movement toward wholeness, one action at a time.

Light doesn't just return to you; you return to it—through service, through purpose, through the daily act of showing up. We move forward not because the darkness disappears, but because the people watching us need to see what it looks like to walk through it.

TACTICAL TAKEAWAY

Protect. Pass. Reorient.

Protect
Guard the light that got you here. Protect your integrity, your faith, your discipline, and your sense of purpose like mission-critical equipment.

Pass
Share what you've learned. Pass the light to someone who's still in the dark. Leadership isn't about carrying it all alone—it's about creating other torchbearers.

Reorient
When the mission shifts, so must your map. Take a tactical pause. Ask: *What's my next best action that is aligned with my vision, mission, and values?* Then take it.

LIGHT IT FORWARD

THE LIGHT THAT carried me through war, loss, and locker rooms didn't come easy. It's been tested, dimmed, and nearly gone out more times than I'd ever admit. But every time it flickered, I fought for it—because somewhere deep down, I knew it was worth fighting for. Sometimes not for me but for someone else.

That light didn't just come from inside. It came from the ones who stood shoulder to shoulder when I couldn't stand alone. It came from the players who showed up broken but still laced their shoes. And it came from God, who kept showing up too—steady, quiet, and unwilling to leave.

So, no, the light isn't mine to keep. It's part of something bigger—something forged in the space between breaking and becoming. It belongs to anyone brave enough to pick it up and turn it on again when the world goes dark.

And if you've made it here—through these pages, through the ache and reflection they stirred—you've done your own work too. It might have hurt a little. But maybe that's how healing begins: when we bring the pain into the light together.

Wherever you stand—on a field, in a classroom, at a podium, or behind a badge—someone's watching for your glow.

So hold it high. Pass it forward. And when you can't see what's ahead, keep moving anyway. Because sometimes the light doesn't just guide you—it grows in you.

And that's how the next one finds their way.

If you do nothing else after this book, light it forward.

Shine it into your home, your team, your community.

Be the steady beam that helps someone else find their next best step in the dark.

That is how we lead.

That is how we heal.

That is how we move forward—together.

ACKNOWLEDGMENTS

T HIS BOOK WASN'T written alone—it was lived, carried, and collected over years that stretched across oceans, sidelines, and seasons of life. It started as a thought swimming in the Red Sea and grew through convoys and classrooms, locker rooms and late-night drives, moments of loss and glimpses of grace.

Every page was shaped by the people who stood beside me—in uniform, in coaching gear, and in friendship—when the light flickered and the fight felt heavy. You carried me through many years of becoming, of questioning, of rebuilding.

To everyone who prayed, listened, led, challenged, or simply stayed— you're part of this story.

To my wife—the best teammate I have ever had and the ultimate safe place. There is no version of me worth sharing with the world without you. You've seen every side of this journey—the broken, the rebuilding, and the brave. You've held the line when I couldn't, loved me when I was hard to love, and reminded me what home feels like when the world feels heavy. You've carried the quiet weight behind the scenes—late nights, long seasons, and all the moments when brokenness took the best parts of me from you—and somehow, you stood steady in every season. You are the heart behind the fight and the calm behind the storm. You are my joy, my balance, and my safest place. I choose you—and I always will. *Team JB.*

To my soldiers, players, and students—thank you for giving me grace through my grief and for being part of my pride and joy in the good that came through grit. Serving you has been both my purpose and my passion. Even when I failed, you gave me a life worth living and made it safe to fail forward. My pride in watching you grow, fight forward, and soar is one of the greatest gifts in life.

To my parents—my mom was the first to teach me to walk in faith, and my father was my very first and favorite coach. You supported me and prayed for me through every step of my career. There is no foundation for this book without your seeds, support, and love.

To Monte Mills and Bob Wager—for two strangers who have never met to be placed on the same line may seem strange, but they were with me in my foxhole in different seasons of life. I still don't know how God decided to place two of the best leaders on earth right in my path when I needed to see leadership excellence the most. I had an absolute competitive advantage with each of you in my foxhole—Monte Mills in combat and Bob Wager in coaching. I am not the leader I am today in my respective fields without either of you.

To my battle buddies—there is no way to name twenty years of friendships that filled my tank and are part of this book. The 302nd Military Police Company. You will always be my home. Shoutouts to the 366th MP CO and the 607th MP BN for their impact and influence on my life as well. Julie B, your commitment to friendship and your willingness to show up with truth instead of judgment came at the perfect season of my life. You taught me what it means to be an unapologetically strong female leader. *The Tough Guys*—Gibby, Escamilla, Dot, and Ordaz— we were just kids at war, patting our pockets and laughing at things no one should ever have to. Thank you for helping me shine in the storm and for filling my heart with laughter when the world around us was anything but funny. You were my light in the chaos.

To my many foxhole friends—the ones who stood patiently beside me through moral injury, grief, pain, and struggle, and let me see myself through your eyes until I could finally love myself again—thank you for staying, for believing, for sharing wisdom and lessons, and for reminding me that healing isn't something you do alone. A special shoutout to *Micah* for understanding me in every season and being one of my biggest supporters on earth, no matter how I was showing up.

To my coaching staffs—sometimes there isn't a word big enough for *team*. I may hold the title of head coach, but what a beautiful family God has blessed me with. My confidants. My circle. My people. God knew I needed you so I could keep serving kids. I still don't know how I ended up with so many incredible humans in my corner, but I do know this—I wouldn't have made it through many days without you. From *Slagle,* who helped me navigate hard transitions and new challenges with belly laughs and a no-excuses, "get better" mentality, to *JT,* who wrapped me in a hug as I broke down in the fog of a cancer season—you made sure I was never alone. The roots of this coaching tree run deep: *Bethany (BG), Beck, and Ridley*—your steady presence has kept me grounded and reminded me why I do what I do. There are too many others to list, but these words and this book wouldn't exist if you hadn't refused to let me fizzle out of my purpose. Thank you for standing with me in the hard days, for believing in the mission, and for helping me keep my light on.

To the Texas High School Coaches Association (THSCA)—your belief in me and the platform you've given me to speak and connect with coaches has both filled my tank and given me a home to pour into. Those relationships and opportunities sparked my desire to serve coaches in the dark and shaped the work I do today.

To the Creighton Interdisciplinary Leadership Studies Program and Cohort #64, The Jay Team—you've pushed me and believed in me. The transformation of growth and belief through this journey with you all has given me space and support to stretch into who I am in this work.

To some of my favorite inspirational seed planters—Jon Gordon, Damon West, Dr. Jim Brennan, Admiral William McRaven, Ed Mylett, Brené Brown, and Stephen Mackey. Thank you for modeling the way in your writing, research, speaking, and leadership—and for showing me that words, spoken or written, can change lives. You have all forever impacted mine.

Thank you to every "no" along the way. Each one reminded me that God's plan is greater than mine—and that sometimes a no is necessary to make space for the real work, the right pivot, or the next path forward.

And finally, to every leader, teacher, coach, first responder, parent, or warrior who has kept leading while bleeding, my admiration for you and my desire to see you keep shining your light in dark spaces is why I wrote this. May you always find the courage to turn your light back on, even in the dark. What you do matters, even when you can't see it.

ABOUT THE AUTHOR

BROOKE BRITTAIN is a combat veteran, coach, and campus athletic coordinator known for her ability to lead others through challenges with courage, grit, and heart. A retired sergeant first class in the US Army Military Police Corps, she served three overseas deployments to Iraq and throughout the CENTCOM theater, earning the Bronze Star, Meritorious Service Medal, and the Order of the Marechaussee (Silver) for a career forged in the extremes of war—where leadership meant courage, clarity, and care for those beside her.

In addition to two decades in uniform, Brooke brings her mission mindset to Texas high school athletics, where she has spent more than eighteen years building teams, mentoring coaches, and leading through both victory and heartbreak on and off the court. As a campus athletic coordinator at Mansfield High School, she has become known for cultivating cultures rooted in integrity, discipline, and human connection—principles she believes are as essential in locker rooms as they are in combat zones.

Her coaching and military experiences collide at the intersection of trauma, leadership, and purpose—a space she explores both in her writing and in her doctoral research at Creighton University. Her dissertation, *Between Grief and Grit: A Phenomenological Study of High School Coaches Leading Through Violent Loss*, investigates how coaches carry others through tragedy while quietly managing their own.

As a respected coach in Texas high school athletics, Brooke was selected by the Texas High School Coaches Association (THSCA) and currently serves as a representative on the Basketball Advisory Committee. She is a frequent speaker for coaching clinics, leadership summits, and professional development events, sharing stories and tools for leaders who serve from the front lines of education, athletics, and crisis. She believes the best leadership doesn't come from theory—it comes from people who've been in the trenches and come back to share what they learned on the other side of adversity.

She lives in Texas with her wife, Jessica, where she continues to coach, mentor coaches, write, and develop their leadership consulting firm, Code Three Leadership Partners.

ENDNOTES

1. Amy Wenzel, Gregory K. Brown, and Bradley E. Karlin, Cognitive Behavioral Therapy for Depression in Veterans and Military Servicemembers: Therapist Manual (Washington, DC: U.S. Department of Veterans Affairs, 2011).

2. This framework reflects my personal application of concepts aligned with the "Three C's" of Cognitive Behavioral Therapy (CBT). I found myself using this language as a leader long before I had formal exposure to CBT literature. When I later encountered the framework described by Wenzel, Brown, and Karlin, it gave structure and language to practices I had already been living. The terminology used here represents my own adaptation for leadership contexts, not a claim of originality.

3. Richard H. Ackerman and Pat Maslin-Ostrowski, *The Wounded Leader: How Real Leadership Emerges in Times of Crisis* (Jossey-Bass, 2004).

4. Margaret Stroebe and Henk Schut, "The Dual Process Model of Coping with Bereavement: Rationale and Description," *Death Studies* 23, no. 3 (1999): 197–224, https://doi.org/10.1080/074811899201046.

5. Kendra Cherry, "Negative Bias: Why We're Hardwired for Negativity," Verywell Mind, last updated November 13, 2023, https://www.verywellmind.com/negative-bias-4589618.

6. C. Todd Lopez, "Former POW Now Leading Advocate for Resilience Training," *Army News Service*, September 16, 2010, https://www.army.mil/article-amp/45312/former_pow_now_leading_advocate_for_resilience_training.

7. Martha Beck, *Beyond Anxiety: Curiosity, Creativity, and Finding Your Life's Purpose* (Penguin Press, 2025).

8. Chris Lowney, *Heroic Leadership: Best Practices from a 450-Year-Old Company That Changed the World,* (Loyola Press, 2005).

9. Elaine Hatfield, John T. Cacioppo, and Richard L. Rapson, "Emotional Contagion," *Current Directions in Psychological Science* 2, no. 3 (June 1, 1993): 96–99, doi:10.1111/1467-8721.ep10770953.

10. Philip G. Zimbardo, "Deindividuation Psychology: Definition, History, and Examples," *Zimbardo.com*, accessed October 29, 2025, https://www.zimbardo.com/deindividuation-psychology-definition-history-examples/.

11. Solomon E. Asch, "Conformity Experiments," *A Dictionary of Psychology*, 4th ed., edited by Andrew M. Colman (Oxford University Press, 2015), https://doi.org/10.1093/acref/9780199657681.001.0001.

12. US Army, "The Army Values," accessed October 16, 2025, https://www.army.mil/values/.

13. https://www.merriam-webster.com/dictionary/integrity.

14. US Department of Veterans Affairs, National Center for PTSD, "Moral Injury," accessed October 16, 2025, https://www.ptsd.va.gov/professional/treat/cooccurring/moral_injury.asp.

15. Brett T. Litz et al., "Moral Injury and Moral Repair in War Veterans: A Preliminary Model and Intervention Strategy," *Clinical Psychology Review* 29, no. 8 (2009): 695–706, https://doi.org/10.1016/j.cpr.2009.07.003

16. Eric Greitens, *Resilience: Hard-Won Wisdom for Living a Better Life* (Houghton Mifflin Harcourt, 2015).

17. Jim Brennan, *The Art of Becoming Oneself* (Balboa Press, 2020). Selected ideas and language are attributed in text.

18. Edward Dale Davis, *Hall of Valor—Military Times*, accessed October 16, 2025, https://valor.militarytimes.com/recipient/recipient-23414/.

19. Angela Duckworth, *Grit: The Power of Passion and Perseverance* (Scribner, 2016).

20. Martin E. P. Seligman, *The Hope Circuit: A Psychologist's Journey from Helplessness to Optimism* (PublicAffairs, 2018).

21. Richard G. Tedeschi and Lawrence G. Calhoun, "Posttraumatic Growth: Conceptual Foundations and Empirical Evidence,"

Psychological Inquiry 15, no. 1: 1–18, https://doi.org/10.1207/s153
27965pli1501_01.

22.   Martin E. P. Seligman, *Flourish: A Visionary New Understanding of Happiness and Well-Being* (Free Press, 2011).

23.   Martin E. P. Seligman, "Building Resilience," in *HBR's 10 Must Reads on Mental Toughness* (Harvard Business Review Press, 2014), 43–55.

24. Jon Gordon, *The Energy Bus: 10 Rules to Fuel Your Life, Work, and Team with Positive Energy* (John Wiley & Sons, 2007).

25.   Seligman, *Flourish.*

26. "Post-Traumatic Stress Disorder (PTSD)—Symptoms & Causes," Mayo Clinic, August 16, 2024, https://www.mayoclinic.org/diseases-conditions/post-traumatic-stress-disorder/symptoms-causes/syc-20355967.

27.   Tedeschi and Calhoun, "Posttraumatic Growth."

28.   "What Is Stress Vomiting?" Charlie Health, June 16, 2025, https://www.charliehealth.com/post/the-link-between-stress-and-vomiting.

29.   Ana Gotter, "Box Breathing: How to, Benefits, and Tips," Healthline, updated February 4, 2025, https://www.healthline.com/health/copd/box-breathing.

30. Seligman, *The Hope Circuit.*

31. "Post-traumatic Stress Disorder (PTSD)—Symptoms & Causes."

32. "Post-traumatic Stress Disorder (PTSD)—Symptoms & Causes."

33. Point Guard College (PGC), "Next Best Action Players (NBA Players)" in-person curriculum session presented at PGC Basketball, 2018.